SHIVERING IN A PAPER GOWN

Breast Cancer and
Its Aftermath: An Anthology

Edited by Meaghan Calcari Campbell,
Laurie Hessen Pomeranz, and
Doreenda Ziba

"…as if, all along, you had thought the end point
might be a city with golden towers, and cheering crowds,
and turning the corner at what you thought was the end
of the road, you found just a simple reflection,
and a clear revelation beneath the face looking back
and beneath it another invitation, all in one glimpse:
like a person or a place you had sought forever,
like a bold field of freedom that beckoned you beyond;
like another life, and the road—the road still stretching on."

— David Whyte, "Santiago" from
Pilgrim: Poems by David Whyte

Contents

Introduction   1
Meaghan Calcari Campbell

I.   BODY

After a Walk to Muir Beach   11
DM
Seizing Control   12
Roxanne Cohen
Dear Body – Love, Mind   16
Wendy Donner
Breasts That Are Not Breasts   20
Rebecca J. Hogue
For Real?   22
Marla Stein
Pat Down   24
Nola Agha
Remodel   30
Jenni Mork

II.   MEDICINE AND TREATMENT

Instructed   40
DM
Cathy Chemo   41
Wendy Donner
Lexapro   43
Erin Williams Hyman and Laurie Hessen Pomeranz
The Long Game   45
Wendy Donner

III.   MIND AND ATTITUDE

It's Only a Year   51
Elodia Villaseñor
Spring Cleaning…..in September   56
Andrea Ghoorah Sieminski

Aftermath: A Marathon 58
  Emily Kaplan
Guided Imagery "A-ha" 59
  Laura Pexton
Cancer Versus Humanity 61
  Judith Basya
Cognitive Dissonance 66
  Lochlann Jain
My Guiding Light 69
  Ariana E. Nash
Holding Both 73
  Sarah Haberfeld de Haaff
Unfiltered 76
  Cat Huegler

IV. RELATIONSHIPS

Cancer 80
  Lochlann Jain
Leather 81
  Meaghan Calcari Campbell
Bomb Shelter 85
  Kristen Nicole Zeitzer
Against Invulnerability 90
  Erin Williams Hyman
Like Mother, Like Daughter 94
  Nancy Fawson

V. REBIRTH

Escape Fantasy 100
  Laurie Hessen Pomeranz
Hurricane, Rainbow 114
  Afroz Subedar
Landing 119
  Anandi Wonder
The Necklace 123
  Robin Bruns Worona

VI.   POST-TRAUMA

Accidental Buddhist   131
   Lochlann Jain
Boxes   132
   Meaghan Calcari Campbell
Fighting Words   136
   Doreenda Ziba
Fuck Silver Linings and Pink Ribbons   141
   Lori Wallace
Am I Doing It Right?   144
   Meaghan Calcari Campbell
Not Pink   147
   Jessica Les

VII. POST-SCRIPT

A Choice   154
   Emily Kaplan
Sarah   155
   Emily Kaplan
Ennui, Part I and II   156
   IPJ
Elegy for Lenore   160
   Erin Williams Hyman
A Life Well-Lived   166
   MEF

VIII. EPILOGUE

The Feast   169
   Ann Kim

Contributor Profiles   175

Acknowledgments   186

Introduction

Meaghan Calcari Campbell

"You have cancer."

Three words dropped into your young, vibrant and healthy existence. Your life is never the same. The team of doctors and nurses coaching you through your full-contact advanced cancer degree, the friends who enter because of love and those who exit because the trauma is too much, the physical assaults leaving visible and invisible scars, the mental hamster wheel churning out unanswerable questions about what cancer will next give or take away from you, the billions of your healthy cells pulsing together yearning to live, to make it, to defy the statistics.

It is a united states of confusion, fear, and discovery.

For some, the aftermath of cancer starts immediately upon hearing those first three words. For others, it sneaks in, a shadow extending its reach, only evident years later. There are many stories to tell about the aftermath of cancer—stitching our broken and scarred bodies back into a whole, reconstructing our identities, denying and confronting and accepting death, seeking answers we may never find. Cancer's unpredictable course is its only predictability. And, as cancer is not just one disease, there is not just one way of coping with it.

As young adult women diagnosed with breast cancer, we have distinct obstacles. How do we juggle resting after chemotherapy and changing our children's diapers? When do we show our new boyfriend or girlfriend our surgical scars or explain our chemically-induced menopause or infertility? How do we manage to launch our careers while needing time off work to endure treatment? What do we say to comfort our friends who have never experienced an illness like this, when even we do not know if we will make it through the disease alive?

Our aloneness is, at times, immobilizing. We watch our friends move forward with the progression of their lives. They have children without an oncologist monitoring the process. They have success in their careers without needing to explain a vacancy in their resumes. They go to the gym without fatigue and range of motion limitations. They think with lightness about the opportunities unfolding in life rather than wondering when death will come.

And so, thrown into this cancer morass together, we discovered each other in a support group for young women diagnosed with breast cancer before turning forty-five, the Bay Area Young Survivors.

With the illusion of immortality no longer distracting us, we get down to business. We compare incisions, treatment plans and doctors. We cry and we yell. We laugh to keep our senses of humor so that we do not lose our way. We see each other for who we are—we are not always survivors who cheerfully grace the covers of informational brochures at the cancer center, sporting pink hats and perfect teeth while being commended for our strength and hope. We are not always more spiritual because of cancer; in fact, one of our authors questions her religion for the guilt it heaps upon her and wonders whether there is a God. We are not always "rah-rah" for the pink ribbon and corporations making money off of our backs through their marketing, with another author conveying what it feels like to be bombarded during Breast Cancer Awareness Month.

We compare the surgical scars and contours of our new bodies, reconstruction or not, with one author asking the existential question, what is now on her chest if not breasts, another narrating her role at a kinkster party shortly after her uterus was removed, and a further describing her sense of violation at the hands of the Transportation Security Administration and their "pat down." We explore complementary healing modalities, like guided imagery and meditation, sharing "a-ha" moments in our practices. And, we try to find our "new normal" while recognizing that there really is no "normal."

We provide a haven for each other away from the societal pressure to be "better" simply because we now have hair. We respect each other's individuality and right to frame our own experiences. We hang out in limbo together, not quite sick but not quite healthy. Several more authors regard the weighty impact of our cancer on our family and friends.

We tread around the slipperiness of cancer language—patient, thriver, warrior, veteran, person living with cancer, no evidence of disease, metastatic, chronic disease manager, terminal, dead. In one essay, the author contemplates why the cancer world's anointed language of "fighting words" does not resonate with her. Other authors avoid using the word "survivor" altogether so as not to tempt fate, or because they have incurable metastatic disease and the valiance underneath the term does not feel authentic. We hold seemingly contradictory states and emotions together at the same time. Living and dying. Healthy and sick. Joy and pain. Hope and fear.

We crack open the unanswerable question of "Will I live?" and the answerable question of "How will I live?" How will I put one foot in front of the other? Breathe in and out? Go to the grocery store? Find meaning in my life? Many of the authors examine these questions and teach us through their answers.

The collection seeks to expose the long arc of cancer's narrative and is centered by Robin's story, "The Necklace," and Emily's poem, "Aftermath: A Marathon." They illuminate the vulnerability that comes with a cancer diagnosis and how cancer's treatments and side effects can go on and on.

Together, all of these stories integrate the realities of life, through and with cancer.

More than in any other time in our history, people are living with cancer. Because survivors are relatively new in oncology, the medical community is still catching up. Scientific studies continue to show that cancer survivors are surprised by lingering problems we experience after treatment, whether it is, as our authors explore, a lost sense of personal control or quality of life challenges like the fog of chemo brain. We are often cut loose from active treatment and the protective cocoon of regular care with a "good luck."

Along the way, we write. We thirty authors write for ourselves and our therapy, to declutter our emotions. We write to share our experience with our support networks, our "bomb shelters." We write to create a legacy such that our voices will not be forgotten when we die.

We write for the women who were robbed of the privilege of growing older, their deaths out of the so-called "natural order." We know they did not "lose their battle" with cancer—they went through difficult treatments, ate right, prayed and meditated hard, and had incredible determination to live. Their deaths are not their failures. The more accurate description is that they lived and loved fully, and are gone much too soon.

We think of the support offered by the women who went before and the friendships we formed with them through a shared diagnosis. And we think about the best way to honor these women, with their deaths begging us to develop into the space cancer razed, to hold fast to what we love and cherish, to consider what the sum of our own lives will be. This book is for them, for Erin, Sarah,

Tara, Jane and so many others. May their memories be a blessing. This book is also for you. While the authors' common bond is being a young adult with breast cancer, anyone who experiences grief and trauma, or whose life does not work out the way they had hoped (i.e., everyone on the planet), might see themselves and their experiences in the stories. And together, we can see the common threads of the human condition, in the beautifully messy tapestry that is our lives.

With cancer, we are learning how to survive and in the process, how to live. Sometimes, we have to touch our feet to the ground, feel the gravitational pull of the earth, tap our hands on our legs, close our eyes, breathe in to connect our bodies to our souls, notice the blood pumping through our veins, and observe those billions of healthy cells pulsing together yearning to live. And we live. Together, we climb cancer's steps, yet we do not emerge as healed—we emerge, as one of our authors reveals, "more complex and a bit ravaged, but…beautiful" in our own ways.

I. BODY

"...I learned to speak among the pains."

— Yehuda Amichai, "The precision of pain and the blurriness of joy: the touch of longing is everywhere" from *Open Closed Open*

After a Walk to Muir Beach

DM

My cold skin holds together a place
where the landscape lights up in patches
of ache, and hard dry grasses scrape
each time the thing breathes, tries
to digest, tries to sleep.
Numb in the sunshine, let
the tongue go to sand, the knee creek.
Half an hour forgetting, then for half a day
face and organs in a fist.
Nothing to grip on
the exhaustion fissuring through.

Seizing Control

Roxanne Cohen

I lost my hair when I went through chemotherapy. I bought a stunning real-hair wig. Because it looked so much like my natural hair, people could not recognize that it was not my own. When I went without the wig, though, my tell-tale "chemo look" evoked stares of pity from friends and total strangers alike. Each time I breezed by a mirror, I shivered with the reminder of my cancer. And, yes, the hair grew back. But, the regrowth was slow, unruly, and wiry.

Years later, my cancer recurred, and I had to endure chemo, again. I swore that I would do things differently this time. My kids were old enough to notice, and perhaps even be embarrassed by, my bald head. I was seven-years wiser. I simply did not want to lose my hair. Was it vanity? Maybe. Was it wanting to avoid the stigma of being a "cancer patient" and the gazes of sympathy? Likely. Was it wanting to feel like a whole, healthy person? Definitely.

When I learned about Penguin Cold Caps that can spare hair loss during chemo, I was compelled to give them a try.

Cancer has a way of causing our lives to swirl out of control.

We succumb to the toxins of chemo and the cut of the surgeon's knife; we are forced to rest when we want to be active; we become dependent on the care and kindness of others; and we have no choice but to admit that our health and our destiny are not in our own hands. So, in this one small way, I saw the opportunity to seize some control.

I was anxious when the two bulky cartons arrived on my doorstep. Cautiously, I peeked inside to find a set of eight helmet-shaped ice packs, individually packaged in clear plastic shoe boxes. I wondered, "Am I crazy to try this? Will it work? Can I handle the cold?" I called on a friend to unpack the caps with me and figure out what on earth we would need to do.

We learned that, for maximum effectiveness, the caps are worn before, during, and after chemo sessions, for a total of eight hours each time, so that they constrict the blood vessels in the scalp. The goal is to reduce the amount of toxic chemicals that can reach the fast-growing hair follicle cells, which, like cancer cells, are knocked-out by chemotherapy. Placement and correct fit are critical to avoid random patterns of baldness. Moleskin or cut up maxi-pads (I am not joking) are suggested to protect the forehead and ears from hypothermia.

On the morning of my first chemo, we pulled the caps from our freezer and transferred them, with eighty pounds of dry ice, to portable coolers. As we unloaded at the hospital, the parking attendant smiled with recognition and said, "I know what you're doing—good luck!" We entered the infusion center with an entourage of helpers, my husband and the two unwieldy coolers leading the way. We were offered a private room to allow space for the production. How different from my first chemo experience seven years earlier, when one friend would accompany me to chat the time away, flip through magazines, and massage my hands or feet. It was all business this time.

We knew that cap positioning, temperature and timing were crucial. The details were complex: start the caps thirty minutes before chemo, put the first two caps on for twenty minutes, extend to thirty minutes the further into chemo you go; continue wearing for four hours after chemo; make sure you do not get ahead of the nurses and their timing of the pre-meds; keep the temperature perfect, because too cold could be dangerous and too warm could be ineffective; remove the caps from the dry ice precisely seven minutes before they are needed, measure their temperature with an infra-red thermometer, and massage the caps gently while wearing heavy-duty gloves; fit the caps securely with Velcro straps; rotate and repeat.

It was a science AND an art.

All of this work allowed my loving companions to play an active, tangible role during chemo. They, too, felt the loss of control and the powerlessness that came with my cancer diagnosis. Serving as my "cold cap team," their purpose was unequivocal.

As I prepared to endure the deep freeze on my head, Ativan

helped take the edge off. And I quickly learned the importance of deep breathing and adopted the mantra, "This Is Temporary." The first few minutes bordered on dreadful (think: riding up a ski lift with high winds and snow whipping against your unprotected face). But, each successive cap became easier and I was amazed at how quickly I could adapt. After a while, it was tolerable, and by the end, I could hardly feel the cold. And, the best part of all: it worked.

To most people, I did not look like a sick person. I did not have to be treated like a cancer patient each day. I could pass by a mirror and when seeing myself in the reflection, remain centered. And, most importantly, I had an opportunity to direct a piece of my present and future. The satisfaction that I gained from being proactive was priceless. Together with my team, we went to the mat against chemo-induced hair loss, and by extension, against cancer. We seized control, and we won.

Dear Body – Love, Mind

Wendy Donner

Dear Body,

As we march together toward the big day, I thought it might be helpful to huddle up. We have been joined as one for a little over forty-two years and, I'd say, have been a pretty phenomenal team. I realize, however, that I haven't often spoken directly to you with intention, while you talk to me pretty much all the time through sensations of pleasure, pain, fatigue, hunger, thirst and desire. So here goes, my first formal letter you.

I want to start with some appreciations. Thank you for healing the scrapes and cuts of our childhood and for tolerating the soccer goalie dives that left your hipbones raw and bloody each August through December. Thank you, body, for being so very strong, for climbing mountains, swimming seas, and running one damp D.C. marathon. You must have been relieved when I entered my twenties and took up yoga; we became really close then, and you got to sweat, purge, stretch and strengthen without pummeling your joints and connective parts. Most recently, you rode up mountains on our bike, pumping like a machine, rarely complaining and almost always ready to push harder.

Thank you for making our babies; for serving up two perfect eggs and growing those delicious children inside of you. Thank you for knowing just what to do during the long nine-month stretches, for opening up to let those babies out, and for making more milk than any one infant would ever need. I'm so grateful that you didn't become diseased until after those wonderful babies were born, and until they grew old enough to manage this journey with resilience and compassion. I imagine you had to fight pretty hard to do so. Thanks, body.

And, some apologies. I'm sorry, skin, for that tanning booth chapter in high school. I'm sorry, feet, for each time I forced you into narrow high heels. To a body who needs a good nine hours of sleep per night, I apologize for the years 1998–2003. I'm sorry, body, for the times I wished parts of you were smaller, leaner, higher, smoother, tighter, or otherwise different. And poor, sweet hair, I'm sorry for all the chemicals. It's no wonder you bailed on me.

It has been six months now since we sat in that small, windowless room to hear that the thickened area on your right breast was not actually an infection; rather, it was Stage II breast cancer. Since that surreal moment, I've learned so much about how you function and the millions of miracles that happen within you every day. I'm in awe of the complexity that allows us to thrive, the delicate balance that is essential for health, and the power of science to fight disease. I find myself craving a deeper understanding of the intricacies of your inner-workings and of the various phases of treatment. I wish I could somehow be the one to care for you, that I was twenty years younger and could go to medical school and be your doctor.

I want you to know how sorry I am that you've had to endure liters of toxic chemotherapy pouring through your veins, but body, let's be straight with each other: you kinda turned on me. It's not your fault—the DNA we inherited was mutated, leaving your breast and ovarian cells primed to become carcinoma. You've handled the chemical onslaught as best you could, often speaking to me with unquestionable clarity and commanding, "Get in bed and stay there. Get up only to pee." I listened, dear body, and we made it through.

So now we head into the next battle, one where parts of you will be removed. There's too much risk that your mutated breast and ovary cells will yet again become cancer, so surgery we must face. I hope that together we can let go of these parts, grateful for the miracles they performed, mournful for the loss of them, at peace with the reality that they must go.

I'm sorry that three surgeons will cut into you, marking your beautiful skin with scars and scooping out pounds (yes, pounds) of tissue. I ask that you'll graciously accept our implants, working to fend off infection and heal smoothly. I know your back will appreciate the lighter load, and your shoulders will love riding around bra-strap free.

It's you and me, body, heading into the next unknown. I promise to honor your strength and beauty and to nourish and care for you as you heal. Here's to us.

Love,

Mind

Dear Mind,

Thanks for the letter. You're overthinking things. Our new boobs are gonna be awesome.

Love,

Body

Breasts That Are Not Breasts

Rebecca J. Hogue

I have breasts that are not breasts. They look like breasts. They feel like breasts. But are they really breasts?

When I look down, my chest appears normal. But, my nipples no longer have sensation or reaction. My chest does not recognize or feel its own boundaries.

Imagine what your face feels like after going to the dentist for a filling. You know your face is still there, but it does not have feeling. After breast cancer and surgeries, I look down and see that my breasts are there. I touch them with my hands. I feel that they are warm. But they are numb—just like after the dentist. Only, my body will never re-grow nerves there. I will never have feeling in my chest again.

I first noticed the lack of sensation when I was carrying a box upstairs. The box was light, but bulky. When I held it, I had no sense of where my body ended. I could not tell how much pressure I was using with my arms, because I could not sense the pressure on my chest.

I was reminded of it again when I did a chair massage at the Cancer Center. When I climbed into the chair and leaned forward,

I had to visually check to see if I was positioned correctly. I did not have the sensory cue to tell me that I was leaning against something.

It is odd not having feeling in my chest. It seems as though, for many of us breast cancer patients, our surgeons never mentioned this, and my surgeon certainly did not. I had read about it, so I thought I was prepared, but really, I was not. While not having sensation in my chest means that I cannot feel the horrible wounds as they heal, it is still disconcerting. It is not limited to being unable to feel silicone or saline implants. Having had a flap reconstruction that took part of my stomach tissue to recreate my breasts, my breasts are truly a part of my body, my blood flows through them, they are warm, and yet, they do not have feeling.

The impact of not having feeling is starting to settle in. Eight weeks after surgery, I am finally allowed to lie on my stomach. The first time I try it, I feel very scared. Am I causing harm? Is there something underneath, which, unknowingly to me, might poke into me? Am I tearing open my wound? How do I possibly get comfortable when I cannot feel?

When I ask about what a breast self-exam looks like with flap-reconstructed breasts, my oncologist said, "They are not breasts."

I have breasts that are not breasts.

For Real?

Marla Stein

When he said that he did not see our relationship progressing, I asked, "Why?" "They just don't do anything for me," he blurted about my breasts, continuing to say that he preferred to be with someone who had "real" boobs.

I was stunned, shocked and angered that I was dating and intimate with a forty-year-old man who could say something so cruel and upsetting. I was screaming inside, questioning how anyone could have the audacity to judge my body and the changes it went through in order for me to live.

Even with his apology, I was shattered. His insensitivity brought my deepest fear to life—the fear of being rejected because of my cancer treatments and their impact on my body. His comments reminded me of what I hated most—the "less than" feeling, and the reminder that the cards I have been dealt are not typical for someone my age.

When I was diagnosed with breast cancer at age thirty-two, I went through four rounds of chemotherapy, with my hair falling out, and a bilateral mastectomy to make sure all the disease would be removed from my body. When making decisions about treatment, I felt that having breast reconstruction would help me feel better about myself, confident to date again, sexual and desirable. I believed that being single during the treatment roller coaster was a good thing, as it took all of my energy to focus on getting healthy. I knew that this was not the right time to be in a romantic relationship and hoped that when the time was right, I would find someone worthy of being with *all* of me.

I am on my third pair of breasts. The first pair threatened to kill me and needed to go. The second pair, made with silicone, reached their shelf life and leaked into a lymph node. The third pair were starting to feel right, and I was excited to get on with my life. However, soon afterwards, I felt as if the rug was pulled from underneath me when my biggest fear surfaced.

Now that the shock and vulnerability have subsided, I have come to embrace my third pair of implants as real boobs. They are mine. They help me feel comfortable in my skin and give me the confidence to live fully and completely.

How much more real can you get?

Pat Down

Nola Agha

In the process of recovering from breast cancer surgeries, there are innumerable stages. For me, at its worst, there was the immediate aftermath of surgery with limited mobility, scars—huge, ugly, life-changing scars—and changes in body image. It was the period where even the clothes I put on were a function of whether I could lift my arms over my head, whether I was still wearing surgical garments that had to somehow fit invisibly under my clothes, whether the swelling had receded or not, and whether my clothes rubbed or pressed on sore areas. In short, it was damn tough to get dressed in the morning.

After my mobility, scars, body image, and clothing choices improved, there was a period where the healing was still taking place, although less visibly. It was the period of physical therapy, regaining strength, motion, and energy. Although they were less ugly, the scars were still healing, sore, and affected what clothes I could wear in terms of rubbing, pain, and my fluctuating weight. Motion was still limited, although not in a way that anyone noticed, as it was moderately straightforward to cover up any inadequacies.

Throughout these stages, my ability to psychologically deal

with the trauma and changes was in many ways a function of compartmentalizing. It was fairly easy to get through the day when the scars were covered with little clothing drama, and no physical activity was required that reminded me of my limitations. The shower in the morning? That is another story. It was the time of day I could not hide or ignore the heavy reality of it all.

Once the healing had hit a point where most of the past could literally be covered up, imagine my joy when I could go back to work! For the better part of every day I could think, act, and appear as if it was all OK—until one day I had to tell a random stranger, who had no business knowing my medical history, or all about what body parts were sore, while standing in a public place where any passing stranger could hear about it. But maybe I am getting ahead of myself.

I take numerous trips a year for work, passing through airports where the security gates have body scanners. I "opt out" because after all my body has been through, I am annoyed by people seeing my naked silhouette (which I also feel is a violation of my Fourth Amendment right against unreasonable searches and seizures). It annoys me even more that when I opt out of the body scanner, I am treated as if I am guilty of something: the agents escort me to a screening area, do not let me touch anything, pat me down, and then put their gloves through the bomb scanner. They always explain how they are going to do the pat down and ask if I have any sore or sensitive areas. Many times when I flew, I was post-surgery, sore, and did not want them touching my breasts, so I had no choice but to tell them, which annoyed me even further. Why should I have to tell these strangers anything about my medical history? Since I had no option, I just endured the ritual pat down and bit my tongue, since anything I wanted to say would surely land me in Git'mo for a life sentence without a trial.

During one particular trip through Orange County, the agent screened me, put her gloves into the bomb machine, and it started beeping a positive YES THIS WOMAN IS CARRYING BOMBS. Everyone went into high gear. They took everything out of my bag, piece by piece, and scanned it again in full sight of everyone else passing through the airport—*hello world, yes, that is my underwear*. I obviously knew I was not carrying any incendiary devices, so I just sat there fuming and rolling my eyes at the absurdity of it all. But then, the boss came out to tell me they needed to do another pat down—but this time in a private room with two agents. We went through a ten minute back and forth: "Why?" "You already did one, and everything in my bag was fine." "The agent's unsanitary gloves couldn't possibly have been the problem?" "Why another one?" "Why in a private room?" "WHY?" They had no answers except that it was protocol. All I could imagine was being in a private room with two agents and no one else to witness whatever they were going to do to me. I finally relented, since I was going to miss my flight and be late for work.

In the private room, they gave me the same instructions as for all pat downs except that they had to use more force. The agent showed me on my forearms how much force and asked if I had any sensitive areas. "YES! You CANNOT use that amount of force on my breasts because I have fresh scars. I had my boobs chopped off and replaced. They hurt like *@&! and they look like *@&! Do NOT touch them." At that point, I started crying. I was so angry that I had to tell two strangers about my private medical history so that they would not hurt me. Of course, they found nothing and sent me on my way. I went to the restroom and cried and cried for what felt like hours. Wracking sobs. I spent more time crying in that bathroom than I ever did crying after I was diagnosed.

I spent many months reflecting on the experience, partially because even the incredibly supportive people closest to me did not quite understand why I cried about the ordeal. So what if they had to frisk you again? So what if you had to tell them?

Part of it was that I was angry to begin with. Angry that my options were between a machine that showed my compromised body, and a pat down where people had to touch my compromised body. Angry that the idiot who did the first pat down did not use fresh, clean gloves. Angry that the second pat down had to be performed in a private room where I was outnumbered. Very angry that I had to tell them what was sore.

And maybe that was the crux of it all. I had been open about my cancer. It was not something I hid. But when I divulged my story it was always on my terms, to a person I chose to tell. It was not involuntary, and I could tell the parts of the story that I wanted to—not the details about what portions of my body could not be touched because they still had fresh, red, scabby scars. That forced violation of my privacy (hello, my dear First Amendment, please come join the Fourth here in the airport security line) added to the anger and the indignation.

Another layer was that during treatment, I had not the smallest sense of privacy. The number of times I laid bare on a table while people poked, prodded, rubbed, measured, photographed, cut, tattooed, radiated, x-rayed, scanned, biopsied, or examined my breasts was too many to count. After all of that, it was pure bliss to put on a bra and shirt and walk unnoticed through an airport like another ant in an ant hill. To have that delightful return of privacy forced away just added to the outrage.

Finally, the return to work—the ability to put on clothes and go about my day without thinking about the past—was a refuge. It was so very easy to deal with life when I was not dealing with it. To have it ripped away in public, in the middle of an airport, was the last straw. There, in full view of the world, I was forced to deal with what I had not—my anger and sadness that my breasts were gone, and although they had been replaced, they were a sad, sorry excuse for what was there before.

Of course I still fly. And I still opt for the pat down over the body scanner. But now, when they ask, "Are there any parts that are sore or sensitive?" I can truthfully answer, "No," and not open up the emotional can of worms that once exploded all over the Orange County airport.

Remodel

Jenni Mork

I found him swimming in a BDSM (Bondage Dominance Sadism Masochism) space. I knew that if I was going to fish at all, I was going to fish in the right pond. I was certain that focused action was an essential part of the search and rescue project I was launching.

I received a social media message from some nonsensical name. I responded, "Yes," he could introduce himself to me at a dominant women's party I was attending that Saturday evening. I had not been to a party in three years, having been waylaid by illness, grief, and a hysterectomy surgery for uterine cancer prevention, following my own breast cancer. Prior to all of that, I was a full-time caregiver and a full-time sex worker. I loved my partner of seven years, who after a "journey" with diagnosis, treatment, recurrence, experimental treatment, and hospice, had died from tongue cancer, all within two years. This gave me a double major in cancer, with a minor in grief studies.

The goal upon leaving the house that night was to kiss someone. I had not been able kiss my partner in the last two years of her life. Cancer took that pleasure from us. I planned for this night's adventure with a pregame acupuncture appointment and a nap. I was at once proud that I was making it out to a social event, and then feeling the guilt of moving on—that feeling intrinsic to deep loss.

Upon climbing the non-ADA-compliant staircase with my heavy black leather case, I saw someone I knew vaguely and quickly put my bag down to chat in that amiable dungeon-esque way. Light topics, hungry eyes. The buffet was set up to provide chocolate and protein. I had been to many parties over my kink-time and knew all the components were interchangeable. The food, kinksters and location would change but the desire to be seen as one's most present and emotionally-voracious self was constant. I am wearing a black 1950s cocktail dress and thigh-high boots that are warm. The heel is well balanced. I dress in layers to show the body parts of my choosing. I am the seasoned fashion subterfuge.

I felt a presence nearby and looked up to see this beautiful man-boy standing tentatively at a distance. He edged near the conversation yet was out of the light circle, giving his jeans and matching jean jacket a look reminiscent of ABBA, circa 1977. I saw that he was younger than me and had straight white teeth. I giggled in surprise, as he looked like many of my past girlfriends, short, dark hair and slightly femme in their masculinity.

I quickly act my mature woman self, the dominant. I envelope him in my fecund overflowing femininity. I was on a higher dose of hormones after the hysterectomy, as my body was metabolizing me into a manic menopause. Despite cancer, I have refused to be deprived of estrogen and testosterone. Having settled enough in this lifetime with things I cannot control, I have fought to keep the hormone mix that I know to be my innate self.

I stand to meet him, and I am considerably taller. I see he is nose-level to my breasts. I know that the radiation dot on my left breast looks like a mole from afar. He says his name is Stewart and he is thirty-three. I think about the fact that thirty-three is the age I was when I was diagnosed with cancer, and the after-effects of treatments began, twelve years ago.

I ask him to sit, as my back and heels are now in ardent conversations of pain, because of an osteoporosis fracture of my vertebrae, induced by the chemo, fluctuating hormones and genetics. I start a top-heavy negotiation. A verbal infrastructure of guidance was needed. I find he is limited in his ability to ask for what he desires, due to inexperience and language limitations. He is South Asian. I hear that his sexual vocabulary is from porn. He says he does not want to have sex in front of everyone at the party. I assured him that this only happens in porn.

I look at him through the flickering lights on the floor, not seeing a wrinkle or blemish. I ask to touch his leg, as consent on both ends is to be modeled in this interaction. The jeans are recently bought and stiff. The corner of his modern plaid shirt is of H&M cotton and also brand new. I am letting him believe that he has somehow fallen prey to the perfect mature woman, who listens thoughtfully and is open sexually.

He is surprised as I stroke his leg, gauging his musculature. He is a computer worker, with no low-body muscle development. His posture caves into his sternum, a sure sign of a young techie. I ask about his body and his limits. He, being young and never chemically or surgically accosted, reports that "everything feels good." I lean in closer to sniff him for traces of alcohol and any other information. My senses are assaulted by his overabundance of aftershave.

I lead him through a list of boundaries around my body. It is a sexy game of tease and denial on both sides. Though I would love to have all parts of me sexually available, I am realistic in ability. I cannot remember when my negotiation was not full of subtle denials to protect my radiated breast, arm swollen with lymphedema, and nuanced sexual limits.

I lead him to the playspace, informing him now that he is with a professional dominatrix, and that if he expects other people to have such verbal skills, he could be sorely mistaken, and then over-beaten. He is lost in the anticipation of the forthcoming action and does not acknowledge my words.

I find the spot that has the pool of light and is not by the speakers. I set my equipment out and watch him become more nervous. I warm him up with spanking and light nipple play. He is not a masochist, and I feel he needs skin touch and emotional intensity. I climb on him like he is equipment, and somehow balance in heels on him like a pommel horse. My dominance is physical and mental. He is smooth and hairless. I watch as his eyes become hazy with endorphins. He gazes at me, the open, trusting orbs flecked with brown. I felt myself becoming wet. This was a most welcome response, and was one of my multi-faceted goals for the evening. Just feeling that my ability to have a sexual response was still present was worth the price of entrance.

I wanted so much to be that person whose outside physical self is flawlessly groomed, a contrast with my stitched-together pelvis, fried breast and missing lymph nodes. This scene is all very sexy-looking, yet my four-month-old hysterectomy scars do not like this human jungle gym action. I groan inwardly. I am not even using my vagina, why is it hurting?

The cacophony of noise around me reflects my inside truth. The BRCA gene mutation demands constant vigilance. Breasts, ovaries, uterus, and scar tissue have all been operated on, then subsequently removed, over the last fourteen years. The sixth surgery is now just a paste and stitch of scar tissue and open space. My uterus was the last to leave with surprise physical attachment to my bladder, both organs entrenched with scar tissue. I kept the bladder for storage, but the uterus had to go as it had a cancer risk too, with the gene mutation. The muscles of my vaginal walls hurt with sexual arousal, confused about the under-construction aspect of this cancer prevention remodel. I count this as a win, as now my confused response is still a response, which I will go with, as all progress is incremental and nonlinear.

I return to this man-boy, Stewart, who is proving to be emotionally flat. He did have great hip flexor mobility, a nice surprise and an unexpected departure from the otherwise under-cared-for physique. I wondered how he felt most alive. I was very engaging, yet he had the unresponsiveness of a distantly-bodied self. He lived his experiences in his head, with muted body connection.

I bring the scene to a close, as it is midnight and I am already risking a cluster headache because of the disruption from my sleep schedule. I am a German time-oriented toppy top and heed time limits scrupulously. We sit and talk, drinking small Dixie cups of water, and he asks if he can confess something to me.

"Yes." These moments always prove to be most truthful.

"I am really into MILF porn. You know what that is right?"

"Yes," I say. "Mothers I'd like to fuck." My heart lurches. The possibility of motherhood has also been taken from me by cancer.

"I mean," he says, "I watch it, like, three to four hours a day."

I gaze at him fondly, as he was honest and vulnerable. Yet, the catch and release policy will be employed, as I am not willing to compete with a scripted interaction that focuses on his idea of an erotic self from celluloid. We sit decompressing, giving inconsequential stories of our separate lives. He has returned to his previous senses and appears happy and relaxed. He was stimulated but not overwhelmed. My hard-learned knowledge is that if one makes a person a muddled emotional mess through intense sexual interaction, the time, patience and responsibility required afterward is immense. I give him my number so he can check in the next day if he wishes, and gently graze his soft lips against mine.

I call a cab home knowing that MILF fantasy talk sparks a sadness that passes and reappears. I watch the midnight San Francisco Tenderloin neighborhood, in all its aliveness, and smile. Inhaling, as the kiss of my unknown future awaits me. I hopeful that I will be here to meet it.

II. MEDICINE AND TREATMENT

"We look for medicine to be an orderly field of knowledge and procedure. But it is not. It is an imperfect science, an enterprise of constantly changing knowledge, uncertain information, fallible individuals, and at the same time lives on the line. There is science in what we do, yes, but also habit, intuition, and sometimes plain old guessing. The gap between what we know and what we aim for persists. And this gap complicates everything we do."

— Atul Gawande, *Complications: A Surgeon's Notes on an Imperfect Science*

Instructed

DM

Gown open to the front

This tech and I are old comrades

Hand on the bar

The cold of the machine doesn't offend me

Shoulder down

The whirr of the poison doesn't distress me

Don't move

I feel like a dancer contorted in a still

Don't breathe

Easy as the film rolls on

Cathy Chemo

Wendy Donner

I have been itching to draw lately, and also feeling the need to process the last five months of chemo now that I am done with that chapter. Tonight, I ended up sketching what has turned out to be my avatar, Cathy Chemo. Making Cathy was the perfect way for me to gather together all of the moments between now and when I started chemo and see it all on one page. I look at Cathy with a mixture of wonder, horror, and amusement, because really it is just so very absurd.

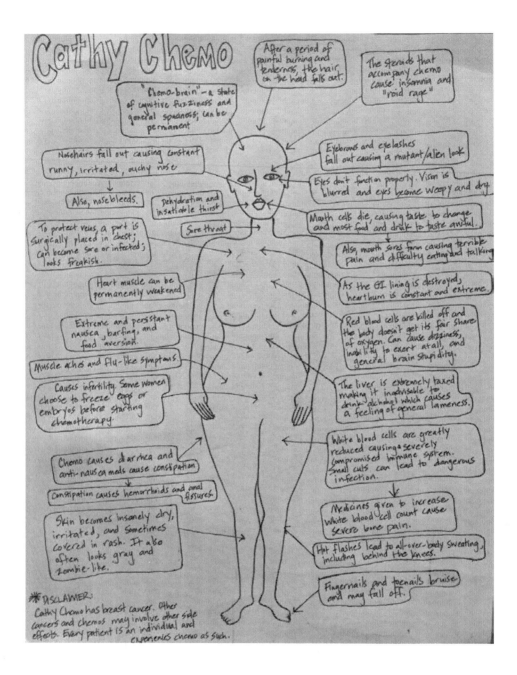

Lexapro

Sung to the tune of "Mexico" by James Taylor

Erin Williams Hyman and Laurie Hessen Pomeranz

Been a year, since that bad mammogram

Feeling blue, now on Tamoxifen

Got insomnia and a labile mood

Crying jags.

Oh, Lexapro

I told my doc that my mood's sinkin' low

Gotta keep me sane in this cancer shitshow

I'll fill that prescription right now.

Get outta bed?

Don't think you can?

Pot's all gone?

Got no more Ativan?

I can't drink!

Oh, yes I can. And I will.

Oh, Lexapro

Never needed you before

Cancer knocked on my door

Now, oh, Lexapro
Bring-on those SSRIs right now.

Cancer sucks, losing your boobs and your hair
And your lashes, and everything down there
That part's good, but the rest of the deal really blows.

Oh, Lexapro
Otherwise known as
Escitalopram
Oh, Lexapro
I'll take my ten milligrams now.

Menopause, deprived of hormones
Dry va-jay-jay and an ache in my bones
Fuzzy head
And I'm soaking the bed
With my sweat.

Oh, Lexapro
My mood is rising
But not my li-bi-do
Oh, Lexapro
I still want my ten milligrams now.

The Long Game

Wendy Donner

I want to introduce you to hormone therapy, the sneaky, quieter member of the breast cancer battalion. Hormone therapy is patient and wise, with eyes on the long game, fighting with brains not brawn. It slips in slyly after its meathead cronies, chemo and surgery, make their big, braggy, bloody show of assault. It steps over the detritus of scar tissue and destroyed GI lining in search of any microscopic, hidden remnants of disease still standing after the one-two-punch.

Hormone therapy settles right in for a ten-year stay, its job simple and clear. It is there to sweep up any estrogen that remains in the body, which, surprisingly, amounts to a significant measure even when the ovaries are removed or no longer functioning. Estrogen-positive cancers feed on this powerful hormone and cannot grow and spread without it. As a now ovary-less forty-two year-old who is post-chemo and a bilateral mastectomy, I am taking the often harder-to-tolerate version of hormone therapy called aromatase inhibitors. Each morning, I swallow one tiny yellow pill that blocks an essential enzyme needed for estrogen production, which, from a cancer-fighting perspective, is just what we want.

I imagine these rogue cancer cells, those with the strength and intelligence to have survived thus far, withering away from hunger and thirst, their estrogen receptor sites like cracked, parched desert. It seems, to me, a miracle of science, the result of billions of dollars to sustain laboratories and trials so that we can manipulate the chemistry of our own bodies. Because of the promise of hormone therapy, women rejoice when pathologists report that their cancer is estrogen-sensitive, a.k.a. treatable.

We women with estrogen-positive cancer are urged to take these pills with gratitude and an unwavering commitment to our survival. We are told that these pills cut our chance of recurrence in half. We are told that the side effects, which range from annoying to miserable, must be tolerated if we choose life.

So most of us do. We tell ourselves that the debilitating bone and joint aches are a sign that the medicine is working. We accept that the drying up of our lady parts at an unnaturally young age is what we must accept if we are to reach ripe, old womanhood. We peel off layers of clothes as each hot flash reminds us that our hormone therapy is skillfully battling on. And we try not to think of our bones that might be eroding without estrogen to keep them strong, and our hearts that might congest because of this hormonal manipulation.

It is an impossible choice to consider life with such compromise versus an increased chance of cancer winning the game. So I have decided it is not a choice, that it is a path without options. It just is what it is, my body's journey through this one life. And if it needs to be sweatier, dryer, and creakier than I had once imagined, then so be it.

III. MIND AND ATTITUDE

"The obliterated place is equal parts destruction and creation. The obliterated place is pitch black and bright light. It is water and parched earth. It is mud and it is manna. The real work of deep grief is making a home there."

— Cheryl Strayed, from *Tiny Beautiful Things: Advice on Love and Life from Dear Sugar*

It's Only a Year

Elodia Villaseñor

Dear Thirty-Three-Year-Old Me,

You will be working your dream job. You will have a seven-year-old daughter, Itzia, who makes you want to pinch yourself (or her!) to make sure she is real. She is funny and quirky and bright beyond her years. She will make you proud with the amount of empathy she has and the love she shares with the world. You will be pregnant this year, and the pregnancy will fly by. Itzia will name your youngest girl Maya. You will add Joaquina as her middle name, after your abuelita. You hope Maya possesses many of the qualities that make you wince every time you remember that when you go back to Mexico, your abuelita Joaquina will not be there, waiting for you with open arms. Your abuelita was many things. But her strength is perhaps the characteristic you most admire. Save some of that for next year and enjoy this time. Embrace it. Hug Itzia extra hard. Hug your husband, Nick. Tell your sister that you love her. Let your Mami know that your abuelita's strength flows through her, too. To you. And that you are all strong.

Brace yourself.

Dear Thirty-Four-Year-Old Me,

June Happy Birthday! Eat that pastel de tres leches that you
so desperately want! Lick the whipped cream frosting off the tip of
Itzia's nose and laugh. Laugh a lot. Place your hand on your belly
often. Feel how strong Maya is and ponder the fact that this is the
last time she will ever be contained. Let Itzia lie next to you and
hug her tight. Laugh together as Maya repeatedly kicks. Remind
Itzia of this and be sure she enjoys the warmth of her mama and
the playful pestering of her little sister. If ever we are not all
together, remember we are part of each other.

July Although you will go through the early stages of labor
alone, please ask for help. You hate doing this, but now is a critical
time to practice this skill. Try.

The first month of Maya's life will be hard. You will do
everything to make the tiny being stop crying. But she will cry,
seemingly, around the clock. You will not produce enough milk,
and will become frustrated with breastfeeding. Nick will tell you to
go to the witch store. You love touching all the crystals and
imagining their powers flowing through you. Do it. Ask questions
about each crystal. This will also be good practice. Remember all
of the words written about the crystals. Jade relaxes, brings peace
and emotional balance, radiates unconditional love and promotes
wisdom. Red Tiger's Eye connects us to our physical self,
enhancing the body's health, inner strength, courage and vitality

and is known for its grounding properties.

Keep a crystal in your pocket. This, too, will be good practice. Feel the smoothness of the crystal in your hand and remind yourself that this is part of being a new mom, part of your process. Tell yourself that you are here right now.

While breastfeeding, you will notice a lump on the underside of your left breast. You will deem this the culprit of bad lactation. You will go to the doctor and have your thought confirmed: mastitis. You will go through the routine of taking medicine. You will try to break down the mass and give yourself bruises in the process of working to break down something that will not be broken down.

August You will visit your nurse practitioner, who you love for her brightness and practicality. You will walk in to the examining room with Maya asleep in her car seat. Your nurse practitioner will enter and you will beam, exhausted, but with the happy calm of a new mother with a sleeping baby. Remember that sigh of relief. She will ask you, "How is everything?" Your response will be the words that change everything, "Great, except the mastitis never went away." Her face will change. She will give you a breast exam. She will be concerned and send you for a breast ultrasound. The technician will call in a doctor for a consult. You will get nervous and Maya will offer an audible voice of panic. The doctor will request a needle biopsy. Maya will be screaming and you will be screaming inside.

September October November December January
February March April May June

Dear Thirty-Five-Year-Old Me,

You will be a mess. You want to kick and scream and throw yourself against the wall. But you will be the picture of motherly calm to everyone else. You will have trouble sleeping and become terribly depressed. You will not want to see anyone and those you do let in will ask "But why? You beat cancer! You're all better." You will have a hard time explaining that you may be well but you are not better.

You will meet a Buddhist ritual minister and attend her meditation classes on trauma. Like the crystals before, the loving kindness meditation will become your amulet. You will hold it close and recite it over and over:

> *May you be safe from internal and external harm.*
> *May you have a calm, clear mind and a peaceful, loving*
> *heart.*
> *May you be physically strong, healthy, and vital.*
> *May you experience love, joy, wonder,*
> *and wisdom in this life, just as it is.*

Just as it is.

You will take part in a walking meditation and wonder why we do not all fall down all the time, because walking is just falling and catching yourself over and over.

And then I remember: we do.

We fall.

We catch ourselves.

Over and over.

Spring Cleaning…..in September

Andrea Ghoorah Sieminski

Today I finally unpacked my chemo cooler—the cooler my husband Paul and I brought with us to every infusion—and emptied the cancer shelf in our pantry. The cooler and shelf housed all sorts of crackers, gummies, lozenges, candies, licorice, Gatorade, Chapstick, and Purell—you name it, it was in there. We always brought a wide variety of things with us in the cooler, because I never knew what would be palatable and comforting from week to week.

I never ate anything out of the cooler. I know we shared our Saltines with another woman, named Deborah, in the infusion room. And I think Paul got into some of the Goldfish. But I did not consume one thing from it. Yet, we lugged it to my oncologist's office for every chemo. Bringing it became more ritual than anything else.

Why has it taken me so long to clean the cooler and shelf? It has been four months since I finished chemo. I was avoiding cleaning because cleaning means I am done with active treatment, and as shitty as that was, it was also comforting to know we were nuking any possible cancer cell in my body.

Cleaning them means I have to start working on re-entering society and the land of the living.

Cleaning them means I have to go back to "normal" life with all you non-cancer people out there.

But, the notion of going back to "normal" life is daunting. I still have days where I'm knocked on my ass. On those days I do not leave the house and I do not get out of bed.

I am scared of recurrence.

I am scared of the unknown.

I am scared of every ache and shooting pain in my body because in the back of my mind, I think it is cancer.

I am scared of my oncologist appointment in two weeks and scared of what my tumor markers might reveal.

I am scared of my appointment with my plastic surgeon next week because I still have a lot of swelling and significant piercing pains in my foobs (fake boobs).

I am convinced I am not normal. Thankfully, according to my support group and the many cancer forums I am a part of, though, none of these feelings are abnormal.

I will take some comfort in that…and get to work cleaning up.

Aftermath: A Marathon

Emily Kaplan

I run 'cause I can
because I could not last year
twenty-six point two

a chance to live life
others were not so lucky
doing what I can

I know how I felt
taxol and carboplatin
one year that week

November second
with my sister at my side
five boroughs two feet

Guided Imagery "A-ha"

Laura Pexton

I decided to attend the Cancer Center's new "Art and Imagery" class. The lead nurse began with a relaxing guided imagery exercise. She had such a soothing voice that I started to melt away. She directed the participants to go to a favorite, comforting spot. I immediately wanted to go to a beach, a tropical, warm, green, lush, heavenly place. Instead, a remote, dry, desolate island popped into my mind.

"No, no," I thought, "not there." Too isolated. Too deserted. Nothing to do there.

But the image persisted.

I was disappointed. "This isn't where I want to be." I thought, "I'm so lame, I can't even do this imagery stuff right!"

These images and this island are just like my life. I do not want to be in this situation. I hate that this is so difficult.

Nonetheless, I kept going with the vision, irritated and resigned that I was not able to picture where I wanted to go. I impatiently waited to see what unfolded. On my dreary island, I discovered a hidden pool with a dazzling waterfall and a brilliant rainbow cascading from the spray. I thought, "Wow, who knew such a beautiful spot could be tucked away on this ugly island?"

I then discovered kind people on the island. They offered me the most exquisitely delicious pineapple I had ever tasted. Wispy billowing clouds floated across the blue sky, making me want to dance in the sand and splash in the water at my feet. As night fell, I envisioned a most magnificent sunset.

"Wow," I mused, "I can still dance on an ugly, desolate island."

"Wow, I can still find joy and be happy in such a dumpy place."

The guided imagery helped me realize that I have get beyond the ugly package that my life has come in and be open. I have to explore and persevere such that the beauty, joy and meaning in life reveal themselves.

If I had not been open to discovery, I would not have found the hidden waterfall. If I had not stayed, I would have missed the sunset.

Cancer Versus Humanity

Judith Basya

In my first round with breast cancer, I was diagnosed on the eve of the High Holidays, a period of reflection for Jews that could freak me out even when life was great. Forget logic, forget science, forget the guilt I'd unloaded in therapy. Forget that I'd been out of the cult for longer than I'd been in it, and definitely please forget that I used the word "cult." Each Fall, between Rosh Hashanah and Yom Kippur, the Orthodox God of my childhood—a strict, sexist patriarch who cared too much about what you ate and how you dressed—resurfaced in my imagination to judge me and reassess my fate. Who by fire, who by water, who by disease—this was the God who'd just handed me cancer.

Back then, my habit when life pissed me off—with minor hassles like traffic or major heartbreaks like the miscarriage I'd suffered that summer—was to blame all the un-kosher food I ate or my transgressions of the most recent Sabbath. Then, I'd remember the rest of the world enjoying their cheeseburgers on Friday nights, their bacon and eggs for Saturday brunch, and move on. I didn't truly believe that illness was something I'd brought upon myself,

61

certainly not by abandoning my family's traditions. Yet with "malignant" freshly echoing in my mind and the confession liturgy on my lap, I wondered.

A brief foray into stripping in my twenties was too obvious, probably. Should I have been more modest about breastfeeding, then? Less cavalier about low-cut, V-neck t-shirts?

Meanwhile, it was 2010, the height—nadir, rather—of the "cancer is a blessing" craze. So pervasive was this preposterousness that even terminal patients were having it foisted on them. But mostly, the focus was on those of us who are expected to survive. I mean "thrive," sorry. Because if cancer doesn't kill you, it makes you stronger. Maybe physically stronger if you wind up taking better care of yourself, perhaps inwardly empowered in a way only you and your shrink understand, but silver linings, think positive, blah, blah, blessing.

Having grown up with the grandfather of this cliché—the version where everything is benevolence—I scoffed reactively and a little bit spuriously. On the one hand, I'd made it to marriage and motherhood, via depression, addiction and eating disorders. I'd learned plenty of lessons the hard way already, I thought, and was tired of spinning adversity as divine guidance. If cancer was cosmic justice, on the other hand, better it should be purposeful than punitive, right?

So I rolled my eyes at the people promising blessings—while secretly pondering what I'd done, against ethics if not against

Orthodox Judaism, to deserve my punishment-reward. Cancer wasn't my only evidence of grace, either. Loved ones who knew about my miscarriage were thanking their higher powers for that, too, since it had led me to discover my tumor early. Doctors were calling me "lucky;" yet even "lucky" struck a chord. I won't parse the layers of circular logic here, lest my head explode. Let's just say that while compunction carried on in the background, I also envisioned alternate scenarios that didn't involve unborn babies. Or my own breast trying to kill me to begin with.

I was lucky because my situation could have been worse—that part was simple. I could discern between real blessings—my husband and daughters, the ends we made meet—and blessings articulated to justify religion or shut down complaints. It got knotty when I counted the fortunes bestowed me at birth. My wisdom and wit. My skin at forty, my arms in tank tops. From a Supreme Being who'd granted me those, customized challenges were perfectly plausible.

In my defense: I'd been raised with the notion that I was special, a member of God's elite, and it warped my self-esteem. But enough about me.

If I total my car but nobody gets hurt, and I wind up with that new car I had my eye on yet wasn't ready to pay for, was my accident a blessing in disguise?

If I'm writing an essay about my loss of faith and five mornings in a row—at different times, on different stations—I hear

Depeche Mode's "Blasphemous Rumours" on the radio, a beloved song by my favorite band that includes the line about God "when I die I expect to find Him laughing," and my essay takes much longer than it should to coalesce, can I blame chemo-brain or is God preemptively laughing?

If after four years of clean mammograms and healthier living I discover a new lump in my breast during Hanukkah—gift-giving season—and it's more aggressive than before and frees my inner atheist finally, what does irony prove?

Cancer is in my family, yet my family is so huge that our incidence rate matches that of the general population. I was surprised by my first tumor, and I was caught off-guard by its recurrence, I suppose, because I'd been lucky…. I was lucky….Why would my luck run out? I'm lucky to not imminently be dying—fine. If my luck holds at its current level, I won't win the lottery, but maybe old age will get me before this disease does.

It's coming for my vanity this time, though; not stopping at a chunk of flesh for the surgeon and a burnt skin offering to radiation. My stomach's been grafted onto my chest. My torso looks like it was bitten by a purple-toothed shark. I have no eyebrows (could somebody please acknowledge my lack of eyebrows? Hello? They'll grow back. I hope. Whatever, I can handle it.). Chemo is fogging my brain, and what chemo spares Tamoxifen will plunder for the next decade, along with my feminine hormones, sexuality, vitality, the sunset phase of my youth.

Hold off the Lexapro (until my liver recovers from chemo, at least): I'm sure I'll eventually, somehow, somewhere find new reasons to be vain. Without my old vanity, though—yes, I realize this still makes me sound full of it—I don't feel special, and therefore, I don't feel guilty. Not for crimes committed against Saturdays. I'm special to my family and friends (even as they lie straight to my brow-less face—also, guys, the miscarriage didn't save my life, OK?). But in the random, unknowable universe where cancer and humanity duke it out, I'm a constellation of dust, unique as any other. Which is unique enough for me—and what I always wanted to believe.

Cognitive Dissonance
Excerpted from *Malignant: How Cancer Becomes Us*

Lochlann Jain

Forms of cancer knowledge tend to push each participant in the cancer world to identify with one side of an equation (objective, scientific, "neutral") or the other (subjective, emotional, "biased"). As a patient, you cannot for a moment forget that the data do not fully describe your life. But researchers and scholars tend to frame knowledge in the abstract, as if it could exist outside of the actual people who manifest it. The power dynamic resulting from the institutional separation of these forms of knowledge devalues the knowledge that people with cancer derive from undergoing treatment.

Perhaps as a result, some survivors respond unfavorably to analyses of cancer by individuals who are presumed not to have experienced the disease themselves.

I have learned this when giving talks and not coming out as someone who has gone through surgery, chemotherapy, and radiation for fear that my personal experience would discredit my views, make me seem less "objective." In this trade-off, some survivors then think that I am an outsider.

Bristly survivors make a valid point. For how *could* you

imagine the scene of the radiation room? The frail gown that had surely covered someone for whom this very treatment had not worked, now inelegantly smothers your unease about the dose the machine is emitting and strains to catch the shiver that threatens to displace the crimson rays from the tumor. The soft-rock radio's ionizing thrum replaces the technicians who moments ago trussed you like a Christmas turkey before saying, "That's probably good enough" and pressing the button to elevate your scarcely-clad prone body higher into the frigid cement vault before bustling down the leaded hallway to cluster in the teddy bear-garnished booth as the machines start to tick and squeal.

I, for one, would not have been able to grasp being an object in other people's daily work lives—a slippery-veined wriggly mound from which to draw blood; a back-wrenching load on a difficult-to-steer bed needing conveyance from one department to another—had I not gone through the experience myself. I will not soon forget the doctor who meticulously peeled and then sucked on each in a pile of Hershey's kisses as he reeled off the statistical likelihood that radiation treatment would work, versus the likelihood that it would produce more and other kinds of cancer. Certainly his view of those statistics differed from mine. Maybe chocolate would have sweetened my end of the deal, but he did not offer.

Experience differs again from an outside observer's social science account of cancer treatment. The humiliation of being told by a group of giggling nurses who cannot put in a catheter that they wish you were still under general anesthetic would not be conveyed by a series of data on catheter implant success and failure rates.

Not exactly predetermined, each of cancer's scenarios funnels possible experiences. From the radiation room to the support group, each new role offers new requirements of physical and emotional discipline, masochism, and passivity. For these reasons, a kind of recognition emerges among people who may identify as cancer "survivors," akin to the knowing winks that parents of adult children give to those quieting screaming toddlers.

In an ideal world, a cancer diagnosis would come with an explanation of its cause and move on to successful treatment. All the small embarrassments could disappear with a bit of psychotherapy if the treatment offered a cure.

Would that I could describe that idyllic situation.

My Guiding Light

Ariana E. Nash

I fell into a dream. It comes back to me in flashes and starts with a young woman in a white lab coat; as we walk through the threshold into an office, she tells me they found cancer. I sit down and think that this is supposed to be when I should start to cry, but the tears that come do not seem to fit the situation. I realize that the woman is still talking but I am not hearing her, the words are soapy bubbles that float silently upward, only to burst against the ceiling. I want to run out of the room into what was a beautiful San Francisco day, but she keeps me there as she fumbles through files and passes me a stack of folders. I leave her office resentful of the weighty world that has been placed on my shoulders. It takes a few weeks to awaken into the reality of my situation; the first days are a blur of teary phone calls and appointments. I think I am going to die, and curse the fact that I just spent a bundle on orthodontics for a corpse.

A week later I learn that the cancer is ER/PR -, HER2+ and I really do not know what it means. Some of the white coats say it is not the best but not the worst, "Sort of like getting vanilla ice cream when you would rather have chocolate." Others say, "At least we have a target." Surgery reveals a small but mighty Stage I, Grade Three tumor that grew to a palpable size in the ten months since my last mammogram. I owe its discovery to retail therapy and a tight dress; I owe visiting a doctor without hesitation to my mother's best friend who lost her life to this disease.

Before finding out the news, I was an average active woman in my early forties. I worked out three days a week and walked instead of waiting for the bus. I was not an alcoholic or drug addict, and contrary to popular assumptions, I never ate an overabundance of fried foods while sitting on the couch watching *The Real Housewives*. My biggest worry had been traversing the trials and tribulations of online dating, where I was labeled "too old" or likely "stuck in my ways" at forty-three. Instead of appropriate matches, I received emails from young men who had been "fantasizing about being with an older woman," or older men obviously in their sixties yet trying to pass themselves off as my peers.

To my surprise, however, one of the side effects of being diagnosed with breast cancer two weeks after my forty-fourth birthday was learning that I was still "young" in the cancer world. I did not understand at first, since society was so busy telling me the opposite; I had felt marginalized since I hit forty. It was when I made my first trip to the oncologist that I understood.

I breezed into my doctor's office in heels, a short skirt, and exposed tattoos. I appeared out of place. In this waiting room, sweet elderly couples whispered to each other, and sons and daughters older than me listened to medical instructions on behalf of their parents. Well into retirement, no one here was concerned with financial district fashion or online dating. During the course of my treatment, the room often grew silent when I walked in, as caretakers and other patients briefly left their conversations to give me "the look," the one that said, "You are too young to be here."

Dating was no longer a priority, treatment was my replacement with its rubber-gloved touches and needle-point kisses plunged directly into a port device above my heart. I concentrated on staying out of a state of depression; if this thing was going to kill me, I did not want to look back and wish that I had not spent so much time being sad. My attitude was the only thing I could control in an out-of-control situation.

Working full-time during treatment, I took three-day chemo weekends, while pregnant colleagues enjoyed four to six months of leave to bond with their newborns. I qualified for three weeks of short-term disability, but as a single person I could not live off of seventy percent of my income and feared that unexpected expenses would arise. Reliant on public transportation, I often stood with bags of chemicals coursing through my veins and radiation weakening my knees as the city buses lurched between medical buildings, my office, and my apartment. There were times I wished someone would offer me a seat, but apparently I never appeared as sick as I felt.

My year of intensive treatment is now behind me. Side effects remain. My once beautiful hair is growing back at a snail's pace with fried-looking excuses for "chemo curls" protruding from where easily-tamed bangs used to be. My big toenails appear in various shades of purple and black. An extra twenty pounds resists every physical effort I make to return to my original shape. My abdomen is bloated as my ovaries rebel in utter confusion.

I wear a new sense of urgency like a shroud. I rationalize that any accommodations I make for a friend, employer or lover could have me waiting too long to fulfill my earthly dreams. The specter of recurrence propels me forward at an accelerated, if not frantic, rate to check items off of an ever-growing bucket list. My keen awareness of my own mortality is my guiding light.

Holding Both

Sarah Haberfeld de Haaff

I have been collecting ampersands. My husband, Greg, just looks at me, perplexed, each time a new "&" sign arrives at our house. Ampersands are tucked away in different nooks and crannies. On our bookshelf in the living room, I have two—one white and wooden and the other clear acrylic, both fairly large. I don't completely understand why I have been drawn to this symbol my whole life, but I feel the connection even more so now. The ampersand represents the possibility of everything—of inclusion, of simultaneous experiences and emotions.

Don't get me wrong. I have nice feelings toward the plus sign, too, but not in the way I love the ampersand. The plus is more about addition and I am not that excited about math. The ampersand allows for the paradox of two or more opposing things, emotions, experiences, to exist at the same time. Not adding one to the other, just co-existing. Holding both.

To me, right now, "&" illuminates that I can have good days & bad days—which can all actually happen in the same day. I can feel joy & fear. I can be realistic and know the odds are not that great & I can still have hope.

I can feel strong & feel sad.

At the very same time.

How can this be?

There are just so many truths that co-exist, at the same exact time! Life is messy. It is not always black and white—or even grey, but rather sometimes it is black & it is white, simultaneously.

I can have pain and nausea & have an awesome day surrounded by loved ones who help me and keep my spirits bright. I can laugh & I can cry. Because this cancer shit is huge and not one-sided.

My former oncologist had a way of excluding part of the experience. That exclusion never felt right to me. I want all the information and I want someone to tell me it is all going to be alright. But she always cautioned against "false hope." And every time she referenced it, I wondered, "What does that even mean? How could that possibly be a thing?" I keep sitting here running all of these scenarios in my mind and cannot think of one in which hope would be "false." How could hope be a bad thing? Ever?

OK, if I am standing at the edge of a cliff and casually decide to jump off, hoping for the best, that would be slightly stupid.

But standing on the same cliff while this enormous angry sharp-tooth drooling hungry beast of certain death comes closer and closer: why would having hope as I took that jump, even given the worst odds, be a bad thing? Jumping off the cliff and hoping for the best in this situation is not so stupid. The outcome might remain the same, but my hope would not be false.

Sure, I believe in science and medicine, and I am not going to give up any of that. And I also believe that there are many other things that can help me heal, things that we do not yet know about. I am trying as many of them as I can. I still have hope.

Hope. Not to be confused with denial. Denial can be a bad thing. Doing absolutely nothing about serious illness and hoping for the best might not be the best idea. But hope & recognition can be a huge part of the healing process.

My new and improved oncologist focuses on my symptoms and wants to make sure I am handling the chemotherapy as well as I can, balancing the benefits with the side effects. As we speak, she often gently rubs my belly; I know she sees the "&" clearly. Instead of walking out of my appointments with dread and fear, I walk out feeling hopeful and supported.

That, I think, is what those of us who live in the metastatic cancer world are looking for—the ability to do what my ampersands teach me: to hold both hope & realism, at the exact same time.

Unfiltered

Cat Huegler

I now see life in vivid color

A filter was removed the day I was diagnosed

The world is brighter, faster, deeper

More beautiful

IV. RELATIONSHIPS

"…So live. Live. Fight like hell. And when you get too tired to fight, then lay down and rest and let somebody else fight for you…This whole fight, this journey thing, is not a solo venture. This is something that requires support."

— Stuart Scott, 2014 Jimmy V Perseverance Award, Acceptance Speech

Cancer

Lochlann Jain

my mother

whose moods I read like

a sailor reads current like

an Inuit reads snow like

an eagle reads wind

now bald stereotype

she jokes

wavering

hairs gathered

some dead squirrel

turning in hands also expression

uncertain

Leather

Meaghan Calcari Campbell

My husband Mike and I just celebrated our third wedding anniversary. Three short years. Three long years.

When thinking about what gift to get him, I did some research and read that the traditional third anniversary gift involves leather. "The third wedding anniversary is often when a couple is aware of the durability of their relationship," as a columnist on marriage.com put it. "Leather itself is durable, warm, strong, flexible, and has a sense of resiliency to it."

This describes our relationship in its finest moments. When my heart sings. When I rise above the societal chatter and I want to shake everyone out of their stupor to show them how exquisite marriage can be, how it is not a minimizing trap or a life sentence.

But the truth is, there are many moments in a day, week, month, year, where the finer moments are more aspiration than reality.

I was diagnosed with breast cancer at age thirty-two, just a few weeks after our first wedding anniversary. We stood together, hand in hand, as the world spun at a dizzying speed around us. We wanted cancer to be something apart from us and something that could not fracture our life together or break us.

And so, we marched in unison between endless medical appointments. We danced in synchrony to the beat of a million treatment decisions. We sang in harmony as we shared the news with family and friends. It was simple, really. We had one shared goal guiding us forward: for me to live a long, healthy life so that we could live a long, healthy life together.

Just as that was simple, the go-forward has been complex. More rawhide than smooth leather.

If there were any flaws in our relationship, cancer has illuminated them all (spoiler alert: there were flaws. We are two independent adults trying to make a life together.).

After the most difficult of treatments finished, we stepped off the cancer roller coaster. We quickly sensed that any solidarity of "us" was difficult to grasp, a ghost haunting our hallways. The adrenaline did not pulse as strongly or focus our attention as acutely—it simmered below the surface, ready to be triggered at a moment's notice and often for the most mundane, non-life-threatening, reasons. We felt hungover, still queasy from the ride. We snapped more at each other. I erupted more at him. The little insults in any relationship—piled laundry, miscommunications and sideways glances—seemed like stomping elephants, open wounds, death by a thousand cuts.

Why? Why, after fighting, begging and crying for my life, was I being a jerk? Why, after expressing so much tenderness and love for each other during my diagnosis and treatment, were we acting hostile, criticizing each other, and during our worst, showing contempt? What happened to kindness and generosity? Our easy rhythm? A clearly defined and celebrated "us?"

We are changed. That is the short answer.

Who is this person, my husband? Is he still my Irish Catholic rock who made me tea to combat nausea, gave me shots to preserve my fertility, accompanied me to appointments and was inquisitive with the doctors, slept contortedly in too-small hospital chairs in between watching over me and advocating for me, coordinated my caretaking when his job demanded him elsewhere, emptied my surgical drains, smiled at me with genuine empathy, and made future plans believing that I would be there to enjoy them? The person I fell in love with?

Who am I, his wife? Is the new, post-cancer me still me, a carefree healthy woman? Is this menopausal thirty-something who lives with countless side effects and now internalizes what it means to live in the present because it is all I am guaranteed, no yesterday and no tomorrow, the same as the old me? The person he fell in love with?

We went through the same thing, yet experienced it completely differently and cannot truly know the other's experience.

Just as I went through the journey of needles, blood draws, chemo, radiation, surgeries, and pills to combat side effects and keep me upright and alive, Mike went through a journey, too. Did he feel pain? Did he feel loss? Did he wonder how this could be happening? Does he wish he could have traded places? Is he scared? Does he miss how easy we once had it?

Does it matter though? Because, he had his own pain, his own loss, confusion, fears, longing for the past when we were naïve and mortality was somewhere over there, in sixty years.

Now, the way forward is a path we must each create and, I hope, co-create. The path starts with acknowledging who we are now, why we love each other, and what our shared story was, is and will be. Just as we invested so much in me and my life, it is time to do the same for our marriage.

Love is more than a feeling, it is a decision and an action that we must constantly decide to renew.

The makings of leather involve blood and death, skinning and shedding, remaking and reworking. As we round out year three, I cannot think of a more fitting symbol.

Bomb Shelter

Kristen Nicole Zeitzer

Breast cancer fell into my life like a bomb. Suddenly. A huge explosion. Deaf with only a startlingly dull ringing in my ears. Everything was a mess. My mind held a chaotic scene of burnt debris and ashy images. I felt the heat of the red flames behind me.

I met with the Breast Health Center's Nurse Practitioner a few hours later. I left with hands full of referrals to breast surgeons, plastic surgeons, medical oncologists, therapists, and support groups; a mess of papers on what to expect next; and a colorful cheery pillow to support my body post-mastectomy. Yet, I still could not hear clearly.

This is not the first time I had to share bad news with friends and family. Twelve years before breast cancer, I was run over by a truck while riding my bike up a mountain in France. I screamed in pain and was numb from the waist down, minus my toes. I was airlifted to a hospital for tests and did not know if I would walk again. After several hours a doctor said, "You broke your back and a few other bones. You won't be able to move for a while. You're in pain, but in a year, you will be OK." While she was not a prolific speaker, I knew my outcome. I would be OK. A smile

85

overtook my grimace of pain and did not leave my face for the entire year. I was the happiest hospital patient in Avignon, France. I cheerfully completed eleven months of physical therapy. I laughed when eighty-year-olds with new hips passed me while I slowly trotted along with my walker. My parents found a way to get me home. Friends helped me navigate the city, and my apartment, on crutches. We had fun using electric shopping carts at the grocery store. My army ensured that I made it to that year mark. I really was OK.

Almost two years ago, I went through a heartrending divorce. My deepest wish for my son—a safe and happy family—was demolished. Again, I called in the troops to help me create a new life as a single mother. My army provided a necessary safe haven for us. Friends flew in for visits. Some helped us move while others organized playdates, took me out dancing, or simply held my hand. I heard the French doctor's voice in the back of my mind, "but in a year, you will be OK." I persevered and within a year I was OK. My son loved his new home and we created a protective community around us.

Now with breast cancer, there is no doctor telling me that in a year, I will be OK.

How could this cancer bomb explode when I was just getting back on track, when my life was becoming brighter? When will I be able to overcome the ringing in my ears so I can hear the French doctor's voice? How do I get through this next year without assurances that I will be OK?

I was afraid to call in my army. How do I tell them that I am yet again in a war zone, but this time with no discernable guarantee to get out alive?

I notified the troops softly and quietly. The embarrassment of the diagnosis and extent of help I would need overshadowed my ability to describe the disaster scene properly. I was prepared for my army to raise their hands in defeat. "That's enough. We have propped you up, been your personal Atlas for years. Time for decommissioning the army." I would not hold any grudges. This battle might not be winnable, and I would have understood if my troops were too weary to get back in the trenches with me.

What happened, instead, was the creation of an exceptional coalition of first responders. One friend researched several surgeons to interview, personally vetted by her professional experience. She organized weekly food delivery and brought me to my first chemo treatment. Another friend searched local cancer organizations for useful information and found the perfect place to purchase a wig. Others traveled across the country to accompany me to appointments, cook, and take care of my son and me—even bringing matching shirts and games to lighten up the mood. Local friends organized playdates and helped bathe my son when I could not lift my arms after surgery. My neighbor took in my garbage cans, shopped for groceries, and went on slow walks with me after chemo. My father did my laundry and played hide-and-seek with my son when I was too tired to move from the couch. Another friend shaved my head when my newly-short hair was falling out too quickly; yet another bought me bold blue hair extensions to make my wig more fun. One friend drove me to more than ten medical appointments, never complaining when my port-a-catheter surgery took five hours instead of the promised two. Soldiers brought comforting food, soothing hugs, and entertaining stories to serve as a respite to my pain and nausea. My mailbox filled with loving cards from near and far. Work colleagues gave me inspiring books and brought me lunch when I did not have strength to get it myself. For sixteen chemo infusions, I never had to be alone. All of it mattered immensely, and significantly contributed to my recovery and healing from each treatment.

Once I became settled into the routine of fighting cancer, the ringing stopped in my ears. I noticed it when at lunch one day with a friend. She gave me a bottle of champagne with a card that read, "Remember the French doctor's voice, that 'you're hurt, but in a year, you will be OK.' Let's celebrate in a year when you will be OK." I had not heard the doctor's voice since the cancer bomb detonated, but my friend, my army, had. She knew what I needed to hear to make it through. It opened the door to the possibility, the probability of survival.

I have always had a difficult time defining success for myself. Am I successful at work if I have a certain title, make a certain wage, or receive enough accolades? Am I successful affecting positive change in my community if I volunteer a specific number of hours or work with enough non-profits? Am I successful if I have a healthy romantic relationship?

Fighting cancer began to identify and simplify what success looks like.

I am successful when I battle cancer and take care of myself to help prevent recurrence. I am successful when I am still here so that I can help my son succeed no matter what other bombs drop into his life. I am successful by raising my son to be wise, kind, and at peace with himself. And, I am successful when I pick my army, or, let them pick me as their compatriot in arms. This has been my steady and beautiful achievement. This will carry me through the wreckage, clean up the mess, and help me hear the voice that says, without a doubt, I will be OK.

Against Invulnerability

Erin Williams Hyman

There are many women in my support group who are mothers of young children. A common thread of conversation tends to be not so much the logistics of this, but the emotional force and impact of being a mother who is ill. It is not only the first consideration when debating treatment options and the primary worry when thinking about being even temporarily incapacitated, but also it dictates how we let ourselves process the experience. One woman at a recent meeting—her first—said she came prepared to cry because she had not let herself do that at home, not wanting her children to see it. Another told me she never let her children see her without a wig. Afraid, overwhelmed mothers want to shield their kids from anxiety and the brute force of strong emotions—but this comes at a great cost. I do not think it does us or our children a service, to maintain this veneer of invulnerability.

From the beginning of my diagnosis, my husband Micah and I spoke to our children very frankly and directly about my cancer and about what they could expect to happen. Nathan, almost eight now and relentlessly inquisitive, asks constant questions, "How did you get this? How long will you be in the hospital? Are there any other side effects of chemo that you haven't told me about?" Still a preschooler, Theo's understanding is more limited to the practical effects, "Who will pick me up from school?" and "If you had an operation on your chest, how do you eat?" (It seems he thought I'd been cut in half at the level of the upper torso). When I first came home from the hospital after surgery, they relished finding ways to be helpful; they even gave me a whistle to blow from bed if I needed anything, and when I blew it, they would come running ("I really should've gotten one of these things earlier!" I thought).

Their initial anxieties seemed to center around the hair thing. They really did not want me to lose my hair, and *really* did not want anyone to see me bald. When I cut it short and dyed it blonde (then various other shades) in preparation for chemo, it was in large part to destigmatize this for them. "What color should we dye it this week?" I would ask.

By now, it is remarkable to me how completely unfazed they are about my baldness. Wig, hat, or bareheaded, they do not bat an eye. We have been spending time at various swimming pools and they have expressed zero reticence about my exposed state. While in Southern California, my four-year-old niece walked in on me unexpectedly one day and said, wide-eyed with shock, "How did you take your hair off? I've never seen a human take their hair off before!" When I was amusedly relating this story later, Theo jumped in and said, in an ultra-blasé tone, "Doesn't she know it's *just* a wig?"

But it is more than just giving them information, more than just realizing they can adapt. I tell them when I am too tired, or when I am feeling down. I let myself cry in front of them. I do not want to overwhelm them, but I think it is important to let them know these emotions exist. An early childhood educator said to Micah and I that we should reinforce for them that "everything will be OK." I respectfully disagree. I want them to feel safe, to feel loved, to know that they will be OK, and they will be taken care of no matter what. But not *everything* will be OK. Some things have changed and will never be the same. I want to acknowledge these things, while still affirming that we will adapt and recover. Otherwise, if we just mask our emotions and pretend everything is OK, how will they learn what it means to face challenges and deal with them? If we put on a facade of normalcy, when they can sense all the cracks anyway, we are conveying that it is better to stifle our emotions rather than communicate them.

All of us parents, struggling with the myriad challenges and losses of complicated living, should not underestimate our children's capacity to discuss and process the hard stuff. Some things we ought to shield them from, but not everything. Just as it is true that if we do not let them take risks, we inhibit the development of their own capacity for independence, if we do not show them that we feel deeply, we are not conveying that there is a way to have and move through those emotions.

One day, in the aftermath of surgery, Theo went to his

preschool teacher, sat in her lap, and asked if she would give him a hug. He wanted to be squeezed really hard, "because my mom can't squeeze me hard right now." As heartrending as it was to hear that, I was also happy that he was able to recognize what he needed emotionally, and to ask for it. I consider that a victory.

Like Mother, Like Daughter

Nancy Fawson

When my five-year old daughter Sidney and I are together, someone inevitably remarks on how similar we look. "She could be your twin," they gush, smiling. People have been saying this about us since she was born and since that day, I have been quick to point out our differences. Sidney's hair is lighter and less curly than mine, her complexion fairer, more like her father's. But this morning, as I watch her practicing her ballet steps through the foggy shower door, it is undeniable that she is the spitting image of me and my heart sinks into my stomach.

It is not that I do not want her to look like me. My fear is that because she *does* look like me, and even sounds like I did when I was a kid, she will be like me on a cellular level. When I was six-years-old, my mother died of breast cancer. This after having a bilateral mastectomy along with other, equally terrible cancer-fighting treatments. And now, thirty-five years later, I am faced with a similar diagnosis and treatment plan.

Having my breasts removed because of disease has always seemed so barbaric—an affront, not just to my body, but to the core of my femininity. My entire life I have feared and dreaded cancer. While it has not always been at the forefront of my thoughts, cancer has always been with me, hiding out in the deep recesses of my mind. Until now. When I got the call from my doctor after a recent mammogram I was not surprised. "It's here." I thought. I am lucky; the doctor found it early and my prognosis is good, but just like my mother, I will lose both breasts.

I am consumed by worry. I worry about all of the usual things that a person in my position would: my children, my husband, the housework. Then, of course, I think about how my body will be forever changed after the mastectomies. What will my new breasts look and feel like? What will my husband think of my scarred and altered body? Most of all, what will Sidney's path be?

When I was a kid, people often spoke about how far medicine will have come by the time I grow up; how I will not have to face the same choices as my mother did if I ever got cancer because "they" will have found a cure for it by then. I peer down at my breasts in the shower and think about the fact that, over three decades later, I am going to have the same hideous procedure done to me as my mother had done to her. "They" still have not found a better way to deal with this type of cancer, and at this moment it is nearly impossible for me to think about Sidney and not fear that "they" still may not have found a better way to deal with this dreadful disease three decades from now.

I know that I am not my mother and, though we may look alike, my daughter is not me. I know this and I force myself to remember that truth. I cling desperately to the fact that just because Sidney may appear to be a carbon copy of me, on a cellular level, we are not the same. She has her own unique combination of DNA; part from me and part from her father. Our matching freckles do not necessarily mean that we have the same roadmap in life. I take a deep breath and try to let go of the anxiety, fear and guilt that I feel for possibly passing along this destiny to my daughter. For better or worse, she will have her own struggles and I try to take solace in that.

I continue to watch Sidney through the shower door as she leaps confidently into the air making up dance steps as she goes along. She loses her balance and falls and when I step out of the shower to help her up, she looks at me and smiles a completely carefree and happy smile, which looks just like my smile when I was her age.

V. REBIRTH

"1. Attempt what is not certain.

Certainty may or may not come later."

— Richard Diebenkorn, "Notes to myself on beginning a painting"

Escape Fantasy

Laurie Hessen Pomeranz

We were driving to our son Jack's Little League game when I proposed the idea to my husband Jeff. "Hon? When treatment is over, I think I want to try to go away by myself, just to think and write and chill, for a week or so." Being the most understanding and supportive man I know, he did not skip a beat before saying, "That sounds like a great idea. You need something good to look forward to when you finish."

As I think back, it was really my husband who could have used a week to himself after all he had managed. It had been a grueling nine months for him, too. Along with all of the fears that came with the biopsies, the breast cancer diagnosis, the MRIs, body scans, chemotherapy and knives at my breast, Jeff was working full-time, doing the vast majority of the care for seven-year-old Jack and me, and handling all of our household tasks, while navigating the sleepless nights we spent as I tweaked and thrashed on pre-chemo steroids and soaked the bed and flung-off layers with hot flashes. He was riding front-seat on the crazy train with a moody, sweaty wife who had been slammed into "acute" chemo-induced menopause. There was nothing "cute" about it, though. It was not what we saw coming. Not at forty-one, at least.

Yes, I would go away. By myself. No organized retreat at a center where they tell me when meals are being served, when it is time for meditation, or to come to the yoga mat. I wanted to take full control of my time and activities. I would eat, meditate and practice yoga at my own rhythm, my own free-form jazz odyssey of chilling. All the ideas for stories I wanted to write that have been swirling, unexpressed, in my gridlocked brain—they would have room and an expanse of time to be fully realized. If only I could go away.

I started talking to friends about my idea and trying to figure out where to go. A hotel? A room in someone's house? A cottage? I wanted peace and quiet. I wanted to feel safe. I wanted nature nearby. I wanted to be able to get everywhere by foot or bike. I would not have a car. Most of all, I wanted to be somewhere that felt inspiring. The ocean. I wanted to be able to see the ocean.

I got online and began searching in the nearby coastal community of Moss Beach. The very first place I came upon looked idyllic. A cottage on a cliff, over the ocean and a marine preserve. Decor was white, slate and maple. Four hundred square feet, intimate. A king-sized bed dripping in white six hundred thread-count sheets and a fluffy white duvet. A heavenly nest. I imagined myself splayed out across the entirety of that massive bed. At our house, it is not uncommon to have the three of us in our queen bed, so it sounded positively spacious and decadent to just sprawl out for a few days. I started to fantasize about the actual SLEEPING. Would I go in the middle of the bed, or diagonally across the whole damn thing? Would I stay on "my side," or migrate to the center?

But, the best thing about this cliff-top hideaway, though, was the huge, sturdy hammock resting on the lawn at the edge of the cliff, with nothing but ocean view. It excited me so much, I knew that even if it rained, I would be in that hammock.

Before going to bed for the night, I emailed the owner to check availability. When I woke up in the morning, she had written me back that it was mine if I wanted it. Oh man, did I want it. Booked. Done.

Now it was time to get back to daydreaming. I had six weeks before I was leaving, twenty-five radiation treatments still ahead, Christmas and New Year's Eve, and the anticipation of my impending return to work after a year's absence. But all I could think about was my getaway. I had to stop myself from packing.

Two weeks before my departure, late one Saturday night, I started. I just could not wait any longer. A bag of books. Twelve of them. Surely, I would have time to read at least a part of each of them, and finish a few. It was a varied selection: novels, and nonfiction about healing through yoga, life after cancer, staying sexy with cancer, and dancing with life's suffering. I would do the reading about cancer that I never did while in treatment. An immersion course in thinking about what the hell had just happened to me and how I might help myself recover.

Next, I packed my activity bag with all the things I wanted to work on. My orange and black San Francisco Giants scarf that I started knitting last baseball season, articles I had been looking forward to reading, thank you cards that I would finally write, a box of letters that I had received since getting sick and wanted to reread. Of course, my laptop would go in that bag too, so I could write, all day every day, when I was not reading, doing yoga, knitting, biking, hiking, cooking, or watching one of the five movies that I also stuffed in there.

Then, the food fantasies rose to the surface. Visions of a bounty of organic fruits and vegetables, minimally seasoned, freshly steamed and clean. There would be kale, lemons, and lovely olive oil. I would eat as much garlic and onions as my heart desired. I would bring a jar of my favorite pickles and eat them around the clock, without self-consciousness of deli-mouth.

With departure-day looming, I began to imagine the clothes I wanted with me. My coziest robe and fleecy sweatpants, fuzzy slippers, yoga pants, my most worn-in sweatshirt and favorite pair of flip flops. I would take long hot baths with the new sugar body-scrub bought just for the occasion and finish off with full-body moisturizing, before snuggling-up in my robe and slippers, whipping up a hot mug of chai latte (I would bring my milk-frother!), and delving into one of my twelve books.

I finished radiation. After ten months of slogging through the thick muck of cancer treatment, I was done. On the day after I finished, Jeff, who is as steady and strong as the trunk of a redwood, who carried our family the past ten months without a whimper or a moment of self-pity, started feeling sick. He came home early from work. He never does that. He did not go in the next day. He never does that either.

I was happy to be able to finally take care of him. I made him a pot of my best Jewish Mother chicken soup. Then I ducked out for my acupuncture appointment. While I was gone, Jeff decided to walk around the corner to the pharmacy. While there, he collapsed. Literally fainted. A kind man caught Jeff as he fell and got him safely to the ground. They called the paramedics. He was diagnosed with a high fever and low blood pressure. He came home, got in bed, and stayed there for the next three days. In the thirteen years we have been married, Jeff has missed a total of three days of work due to illness. Now he missed three in a row. I found it so symbolic that the day after my treatments ended, he toppled over. He had been holding it together so bravely and with such endurance, now he could finally breathe, let go, and crumple to the ground, unconscious.

Then I got sick. Jeff and I were a mess of fevers, deep coughs, and groans. I was sad, fuming and scared. How could this happen? What if my retreat was finally here and I was too sick to enjoy it? I am finally done with cancer treatment and now this? What if I passed out in the adorable cottage and no one was there to catch me?

Then our son got sick. The night before I left on my long-awaited retreat, Jack started getting worse. Monday morning came, time for my departure. My husband was going to drive me to the cottage and drop me off with my bike and my four hundred bags of stuff. Jack was too sick to go to school. This never happens. Our child had only thrown-up once in his life, and it was because he accidentally ate soap. He had a raging fever. He never got fevers. So, he came with us for my retreat drop-off.

We walked into the cottage. Seeing how pretty and white and pristine it was, I was instantly protective of the space. I wanted it to stay clean. No muddy tennis shoes would walk on these pale wood floors. No one would muss up that crisp bed but me. After the unloading of the car (it was embarrassing, really, all those bags of stuff for one person, overflowing with activities and any food or beverage I might crave in my week away), off the boys went, with hugs and kisses and waving until we could no longer see each other. I was alone.

At last.

I spent the next couple of hours putting everything exactly where I wanted it, arranging all my skin products in a systematic and visually-pleasing manner on the little hutch in the bathroom, moving the flower arrangement so that it did not obstruct my view of the ocean. I fanned out my dark chocolate bar selection like magazines in a dental office, and piled my German gummi stash into a silver bowl by the reading chair. Everything I needed or wanted was here. I would keep it tidy and organized, and that would create the spaciousness to be, do, and write without distraction.

After getting all unpacked and situated to perfection, I ate a stinky onion bagel with a side of Bubbies pickles. I heaved great exhalations, with no one to offend but myself. I took a walk out to the marine preserve. There was a great negative tide that week, and at low tide, all the reef was exposed. I wandered among sea anemones and starfish and tried to begin the process of decompressing. And like the reef that day, I wanted to see what was beneath the waves.

Upon my return to the cabin, I got the call that my son had a one-hundred-and-three-degree fever. Then I checked my email (note to self: do not check email within the first hours of being "on retreat"). I learned that my friend, Tara, from my breast cancer support group, was in the Neuro ICU. Tara and I attended a weekly mindfulness meditation class together, taught by a fellow survivor. We had gotten close. At our last class, Tara was not feeling well. But, she had just returned from Mexico, so we were all sure the reason for her deep earaches and headaches was from flying or still having ocean water in her ear. The email said that Tara had just been diagnosed with metastasis to the brain and needed emergency neurosurgery. Tara went to the doctor to investigate the headache, and they never let her go home.

106

Tara was one month ahead of me in treatment. Her hair, like mine, was fresh and new, one month longer than my fuzzy sprouts. She showed me the progressive burn and blistering and healing from radiation, to prep me for what was to come. She reassured me that she was healing well, as I would, too.

So here I am in my little coastal slice of heaven, in full-tilt worry about my sick child, who sounded so defeated and frail on the phone. My heart ached to hold him, love him and wrap my smothering arms around him. My baby was burning with fever, and I was trying to relax in a hammock with a chai? Not workable. And Tara. She was fine a month before and now she is having brain surgery, imminently? She thought she was done, and then this. Are we not supposed to be able to expect a small window of respite before the next cancer shitstorm hits? How can I be here, trying to read a juicy novel, or write some self-exploratory cancer piece, or steam an organic artichoke, when Tara is in the hospital, about to go under the knife?

I put on a Bach oboe concerto, made myself some crudités with a spring onion dip, poured a cold glass of rosé, and turned on the gas fire pit to warm my feet. I read my book with a flashlight, long after the sun went down and the coastal stars shone bright. The scene and accoutrements were dreamy, but my mind and heart were racing with a profound sense of fear and vulnerability.

I told myself that I needed to try to make the most of this precious window of retreat time. No one was telling me or asking me to come home. My husband reassured me that he had things covered and wanted me to take this time and heal, recover and enjoy myself. Tara's family and friends were rallying around her, too.

I went about trying to relax as best I could. I napped, rode my bike, watched a complete season of *The Bachelor*, and munched on dark chocolate. I watched the sun set.

And I was tense as hell. Why could I not drop-down to a quieter, more contemplative space, where the words and tales would fly out of me and onto my waiting laptop? What about the lists of story ideas that had been accumulating on a notepad, just waiting for time and space to be fanned into life? Here I was, alone, ample room to express and unfold, and I could do nothing but ruminate and stir in my own oniony vapors.

By Tuesday night, my son was still feverish and I just needed to be with him. I felt a fierce yearning to cradle him in my arms. I called my sister-in-law and asked her to take me into San Francisco with her the next morning, on the way from her coastal home to her job in the city. I met her on the side of Highway One, like a hitchhiker, and she took me home. Walking into the house and having my long, lanky eight-year-old crawl into my arms gave me a deep sense of peace. His arms were slung around my neck and his legs dangled off my lap. I wrapped him up in a soft blanket and put him in the car, and we drove down the coast to my seaside rental. The plan was for him to nap in the king-sized bed, drink fresh-squeezed orange juice, and bake out his cold in the warmth of the sunny hammock. At the end of the day, I would drive him home and catch a ride back down here to resume "my time."

We spent a quiet day at the cottage. No nap was taken. We walked to the taqueria for orange juice and quesadillas and ate them on the lawn overlooking the ocean. We laid in that big hammock, with Jack's head on my chest, for hours. For a long while, I had been unable to have that kind of snuggling, due to mastectomy incisions, drains, pains, chemo port, fresh scars, and radiation burns. It felt like I was really healing, to be able to lay there so closely, without pain or fear of pain.

In the late afternoon, we returned to the city, and I said goodbye to my family again. I felt calmer just having had the chance to go home, to see them, and then, to renew my commitment to this personal time.

I returned to the coast and jumped on my bike. I rode along the highway, past fields of artichokes, my bike and me casting long shadows as we sailed along at dusk. I felt absurdly free. When I got home, I ate dinner standing-up in the kitchen then flopped out on my bed for a *Portlandia* bender.

Waking up the next morning, I realized that I had only one day and night left. I still had not written anything and had read just one hundred pages, in just one of my books. I had practiced yoga only twice. I had not cooked a fraction of the things I brought. I had eaten only one bar of chocolate. I had not knitted a stitch, nor watched any movies. I did not write letters or re-read the cards either.

The pressure was on. I really needed to hurry up and relax.

To jumpstart "relaxing," I ditched the cozy bungalow and overflowing activity bag, and decided to head for the hills and go horseback riding. I called a local ranch and arranged a private trail ride. It felt physical, without being strenuous. It was so peaceful and gorgeous up on that horse, looking down at the ocean as we traversed the hills of Moss Beach. Grooming and brushing Sally, a "moody mare" as the guide described her (my kindred equine spirit), helped me dial-down my racing thoughts and pressured head. I could feel myself beginning to re-inhabit my body.

After the ride, I came back to my nest and relished a long, hot shower, wherein I exfoliated with my new loofah and sugar scrub. I got rid of all the trail dust and horse smell and then filled the tub for a long, hot bath. Instead of reading, I just tried to watch my thoughts.

Donning my favorite robe and a floppy sunhat, I took to the hammock with my book on mindfulness. Clearly, I had some things to learn. Within a short while, I was inspired but sleepy. I fell into a delicious three-hour nap in the hammock and awoke in the late afternoon.

I checked email and read that Tara was in surgery at that very moment. Feeling the pull of the ocean, I headed out the door.

Opening the gate from the property, a trail ran to the left, and I followed it. It led me to a cliff, where I saw a long, wooden staircase, heading straight down to a pristine, empty sandy cove. I careened down the stairs to the glorious stretch of private beach. No one in sight. I began to practice yoga on the sand at the water's edge. The sand was warm and wet. I noticed that my mind was quieter than it had been. I sat and meditated. I imagined a door opening on top of my head and allowing in a white light. I watched the white light as it moved throughout my brain and body, picturing it cleansing and healing my now vanquished breast, and my chest, still blistered and peeling from radiation. Once my body was full of light, I closed the door on the top of my head, and allowed myself to feel and see my body as a body full of light. Tara and I learned this white light meditation in our mindfulness class. I used it every day on the radiation table. It was the only thing that allowed me to be calm enough to remain motionless while they burned me with something hotter than fire.

Then I did a loving-kindness meditation practice for Tara. "May Tara be free from internal and external harm. May Tara have a calm, clear mind, and a peaceful, loving heart. May Tara be physically healthy, strong, and vital. May Tara experience love, joy, wonder and wisdom in this life, just as it is." Doing this loving-kindness practice was the first time I had felt truly peaceful since I had been here. I was not there close to Tara, but I was holding her closely to my heart and mind as she lay, intubated, her skull open to the scalpels. I was not cooking for her today, but I was holding her in gentle white light. I know she would be glad of that. I would cook for her next week, when we both got home.

Walking back to my cottage, I felt a sweet, surprising stillness inside. I grabbed my radishes, jicama and hummus and a hot mug of green tea and watched the sun set from the lawn. When the golden rays slipped completely away, I read my mindfulness book in the dark, by lantern-light. The book spoke to me about clinging and the nature of desire. Desire is a longing for things to be other than they are. When we cling, we are anxious, self-judging, not accepting the moment just as it is. It is OK, the author explained, to have goals, but dangerous when we attach importance to the outcome of the goals. When we are clinging, we are racing. We can feel it as tension in our necks and jaws. We are not embracing the moment, the joy and the suffering that inevitably ebb and flow throughout the course of an hour, a day, a life.

I came inside. Instead of eating while standing up in the kitchen, I cooked myself a lovely dinner—fettuccine with shrimp and garlic and parsley, sautéed endive and lemony broccolini. I watched *It Might Get Loud*, the documentary with Jimmy Page, The Edge, and Jack White, while I ate exquisitely slowly, at the table. I used a cloth napkin. I drank a yummy Sauvignon Blanc.

At ten pm I was tired and decided to let myself go to bed, rather than feel compelled, as I normally would, to "maximize" my evening by staying up late. I set my alarm for six am, so that I could savor a quiet sunrise on my last day at the cottage.

When my alarm started chirping in the morning, I woke up to find that for the first time all week, I was sleeping across the entire bed.

I made a super-hot latte, flung-open all the curtains, and finally opened up my laptop and started writing. I did not stop until it was time to pack up my kale and head home.

In loving memory of Tara Schubert. Tara died two months after her surgery, at the age of thirty-seven.

Hurricane, Rainbow

Afroz Subedar

"After a hurricane, comes a rainbow," I posted this phrase on social media while in one of my most defeated places in the middle of chemotherapy, hoping for better days.

I discovered my lumpy boobs in my early twenties. After some poking and prodding, I found a fibro-adenoma, or non-cancerous lump in my medically-coined "dense" breasts. This was the beginning of my increased awareness of THE BOOBS.

Several years later at my doctor's office, I complained about terrible pain I would get in THE BOOBS with my cycle. Even an accidental brushing of my own arm would cause significant pain. I went through several rounds of having cysts drained from both sides. Merely seven months later, I felt something out of the lumpy ordinary. It felt like a hard small pea, deep in my tissue. After it persisted, I went in for a check-up. The ultrasound confirmed "something." After hearing from my surgeon that it looked benign and weighing my options, we agreed to surgically remove the lump.

Afterwards, the surgeon told my mom it appeared benign. Well, of course! The first lump was benign. The ultrasound gave

114

the impression of it being benign. So it had to be benign. And I was only thirty-two years old, no family history and simply too young for cancer. Imagine the shock when I got the phone call. BLAH, BLAH, BLAH carcinoma BLAH, BLAH need to clear the margins BLAH radiation. I called my surgeon back on her cell phone, "Is this what they call *BREAST CANCER?*" And on we go.

Over the next ten months, I had another surgery, harvested and froze my eggs, did four rounds of chemo, was hospitalized in isolation for neutropenia, lost eighty percent of my hair even with the medical cold cap that I wore to prevent hair loss, found a benign lump in my other breast, let my apartment go and moved in the middle of chemo, and then had thirty rounds of radiation.

Although doctors warned me of acute side effects and guided me through the treatments, they never cautioned me about what happens afterwards. Upon finishing radiation, I wrote, "I plan on starting a back-to-life, back-to-reality boot camp next week— exercise, nutrition, prayer, and whatever else I can do to continue to get my strength, stamina, and focus back. It is a time of transition where the current me—the more insightful me who has new priorities and renewed strength in faith, love for life and beloved people—merges with the old me. Only I am an upgraded version of Afroz - Afroz 2.0, if you will."

Although I had some preconceived notion as to what the recovery stage would entail, I was unprepared and left struggling to pick up the pieces that no longer fit together. This is the aftermath, as a truthful poem:

Loss of confidence mentally and physically
Robbed of comfort with my appearance and abilities
Not assured in who I was

Physical therapy
Walking, yoga, the gym

Psychological therapy
Mindfulness meditation

Chemobrain
Neuro-feedback

Needing medications to prevent me from losing my mind
Tamoxifen crazy, Tamoxicrazy

Changing body
Achy body

Hot flashes
Night sweats
Sleep deprived

Being thirty-six
Feeling sixty-six

Changing relationships
Boyfriend becomes husband

Changing priorities
Sixty percent others, forty percent myself
Sixty percent myself, forty percent others

Rediscovering myself
Best friends questioning who I am
Best friends getting to know who I am now

Loss of job
Door opens to dream job

Loss of apartment
First time home-owner

Was living in the future
Now living in the moment

Faith
More faith

And forever faithful

Endless appointments
Mammograms, MRIs, ultrasounds

Frozen eggs
Non-functioning ovaries
Questioning dreams of motherhood

Tamoxifen five years, new research says ten years

Alive, in a hurricane
Alive, finding rainbows in the most unexpected places
Alive.

Landing

Anandi Wonder

We are told that the replacement of cells happens at such a rate that we are entirely new, a replica of our former self, every seven years. Our brains have been recreated wholly, our internal organs, our limbs. Yet the gradual nature of this process ensures that we are oblivious to it, that unless we work to take advantage of this opportunity for transformation, we are remade in our own image again and again, emerging new yet unchanged. Unless something catastrophic occurs to upset this delicate balance of events.

I endured chemotherapy by telling myself over and over that it would someday end and all would once again be as it was before. If I could only get through this, I could go back to normal. My cells were destroyed by the millions, billions, with every infusion. My hair follicles died, my stomach and intestines were clogged and slowed by the debris of dead linings sloughed off and piling up, my brain function was decimated as the poisons destroyed my precious gray matter and connections, along with the targeted cancer cells. Talk of how psychological traumas and experiences can change us is familiar territory, but some things go beyond the machinations of trauma and fear. With an extermination of the very building blocks of my body, could things ever be the same? Was there ever a chance that they would regrow as they had been before the cataclysm?

A sickly Sleeping Beauty, I woke in a body that had grown and changed while I was unaware. I did not recognize myself, I did not know where I fit in, was not sure how to step out of my glass box.

The body I had known for thirty-five years in all its chilly, shivering comfort now burns and sweats. Five years since everything changed, I still open my drawers to dress and stare in confusion at the rows of useless sweaters and scarves, neglected and dusty. Heat radiates from my body; I am a brazier of burning coals, a human torch, a sun exploding in on itself. Snowflakes sizzle against my bare cheeks, the glow of me should light rooms. Where I once scoffed at friends in what I perceived as inadequate bundling and forced them into hats and jackets, now I bathe in chilled water and still smolder, ready to reignite the moment vigilance is relaxed.

For thirty-five years, the ocean was the true north and touchstone of my life. I never knew a time before there was the ocean and before it had become the outward expression of whatever unfocused spirituality I possess. I was one week old the first time I was taken to the edge of the land and I must have felt I had been brought back home to the womb—for my whole life the

Pacific has remained a reliable home. A constant, until nothing was constant anymore.

As soon as I was physically able, I headed outside, out of the buildings and away from the suffocating limits treatment had imposed on me. In my new body, I found that the waves were as beautiful and rolling and unfathomable as ever, but had somehow become just another pretty view. The chill waters were a godsend on my fevered flesh, but my soul remained firmly anchored and pragmatic. I sought out the ocean in search of more than mere water or sun, but when I would arrive to find myself apathetic and unmoved, I began to fear that I had lost the ability to be transported, that a year spent mostly indoors had severed my connection to the natural world.

Even as I worried that the independence I had craved for so many months was not enough to liberate me from my confinement, I slowly realized that in fact, something unexpected was happening. The familiar arid hills of California suddenly touched something within me. The rolling hills of dry grasses had become a kaleidoscope of subtle yellows and ochres, the gnarled branches of scrubby bushes profound, the graceful limbs of trees inclining over shadowed hollows a glimpse of paradise. The landscape I had avoided my whole life, that I had fled in favor of the damp coastal redwood forests and wet beaches, had opened up to me and revealed itself as indescribably complex and vibrating with meaning.

I woke up one day and everything around me appeared different, upended; but nothing outside me had changed. The things I see and hear and smell are different to me because I am not the same creature I once was; I had shed my familiar skin, yet it took me years to notice I was wearing a new one.

If a dolphin is remade in the form of a coyote, does she remain a dolphin? Do her piscine habits and ways and thoughts retain usefulness? Or are the vestigial fins and gills hobbles, dead cells clogging her system and slowing her down? It may be time to shed my past and have faith that my new hide will serve me best as I traverse this new terrain. But how does a marine creature learn to howl and run?

I might prefer answers and ease but learning is made of questions and challenges; the process of fighting through these thickets of thorns is living. And I live.

The Necklace

Robin Bruns Worona

Just over three years ago, when I was thirty-six weeks pregnant with twins, my husband Jon gave me a necklace. It was a silver Navajo piece with two turquoise stones, the babies' birthstones, nestled between outstretched wings with dangling feathers. One stone was slightly smaller and above the other, mimicking the position and size of my son and daughter in utero.

I wore that necklace through forty-eight hours of labor, and after that, almost every day, especially when I needed extra luck. My babies, Luna and Walker, would pull on the chain and try to chew on the feathers. As they got older, they loved looking at it and would point to the stones and say, "this is Walker, and this is Luna."

I often marvel at how we cling to symbols when things go to shit. That necklace became my prayer beads, my Buddha belly. I wore it to every doctor appointment during those horrible early days of my breast cancer diagnosis. Shivering in a paper gown, I would run my fingers over the smooth wings and feathers and around each of the stones. I would think of my kids, take a deep breath and brace myself for the next round of bad news. Then, at some point when I had been poked and prodded too much, when I had taken it off for yet another biopsy or imaging scan, I stopped putting it back on.

I had a port put in through which to draw blood and inject chemotherapy. The doctors had assured me it would be barely noticeable and would make life so much easier. But it was disgusting—a painful, three-pointed lump just above the neckline of my shirts. It took months before it did not constantly irritate me, and I certainly did not want to bring attention to it with a necklace. Toward the end of chemo when the port pain had dulled and I needed some extra luck gearing up for surgery, I wanted my necklace. Yet, it was gone.

By this time I was well into the haze of chemo. Chemo was like a nightmare—trying to run but stuck in sludge. It was like my body and mind were coated in rubber cement. Toxic, gooey, slow. Hallucinatory. Once I realized the necklace was gone, I had no idea *when* it had gone. It took me at least a week to be certain it actually *was* gone. My habit during chemo was to let everything go to hell for the two weeks after each treatment while I felt like I was dying. Then in the final week before my next treatment, I would do my best to pay bills, sort mail, return emails, and carry on. I always had piles to sort through—medical folders filled with booklets, pamphlets, receipts and business cards. Then there were the things I collected on my own—flyers, taxi vouchers, hand-scrawled notes, articles, and get-well cards. Haphazard, tilting piles strewn about the house. So at first I was convinced the necklace was simply in one of the piles.

I cried for my necklace. I could not sleep. I dug around in the same places over and over again. I tore through the piles. I hobbled up and down the stairs, back down to the car in the garage, searching under the seats, in the washing machine, everywhere. Finally, I told Jon. He also frantically searched the house, his pockets, his bags. We both awoke during the night from dreams of a forgotten spot where the necklace was safely waiting. But every time our hopes were dashed. We called the hospital, the oncologist, the surgeon, the plastic surgeon. Nurses searched the official and unofficial lost-and-founds. We left our cell numbers. We went in person and asked every staff person we encountered. We watched as drawers were emptied. Nothing. Gone. We played "it'll turn up" for weeks. It did not.

As the date of my mastectomy approached, I talked to jewelry makers about a reproduction. Most were hesitant, sensing trouble if it was not exact. Jon reminded me that a remake would not be authentic and urged me to wait in hopes that the original would turn up. So I gave up. I had my surgery without my good luck necklace. Instead of running my fingers over smooth silver, I gritted my teeth and tried pathetically to do visualization and meditation. I envisioned a calm lake like the podcast told me to do. And I added my necklace, glittering at the bottom, to the image.

When my hair started coming in, I dug out all my big earrings.

I tried getting into lipstick. I bought a new scarf to wear around my neck. But I still missed my necklace. It was almost Christmas. I told Jon I still wanted a replacement and then I told him I was not sure, maybe earrings would be better.

Getting ready for Christmas was hard. I was deflated, exhausted. I gave up on the idea of Christmas shopping. The doctors wanted me to start radiation but I pushed for a break, just a couple more weeks for the holidays. On Christmas Eve, as I was putting the presents hurriedly under the tree so that I could get to sleep, I felt like I was limping to the finish line. But that was nothing compared to how Christmas Day would hit me.

I thought I would be so happy to be alive, relishing every smile as the kids tore open their presents. Instead, I was filled with a panicky terror that this would be my last Christmas. The cancer was spreading to my brain, my liver, my bones, and we just did not know it yet. Watching the kids enjoy their presents was like lemon juice on a paper cut.

Then, I opened a present from Jon. A new necklace.

It is not the same as the old one. The feathers are more detailed, rougher looking, fiercer, more crow-like. The stones, too, seem tougher looking. Yet the chain is more delicate. It is beautiful. I cried. Bawled, really.

Later that day I was sitting with Luna and just like she had with the old necklace she pointed to the turquoises, "this is Walker, and this is Luna." Then she held the feathers, "This is Mama and

126

this is Papa" and for the wings, "Our family!"

The phrase "new normal" gets referenced a lot in cancer circles. I hate it. But when I run my fingers over my new necklace, I get it. It is not the same. It is more complex and a bit ravaged, but it is beautiful in its own way.

VI. POST-TRAUMA

"Straight from the fear of loss I plunged into the fear of being lost.

I couldn't stay long enough between them

In the sweet little no man's land of my everlasting

Passing days."

— Yehuda Amichai, "I Foretell the Days of Yore" from *Open Closed Open*

Accidental Buddhist

Lochlann Jain

Even the
time until tomorrow

a crevasse so slippery deep
and no crampons. Just
you on the other side
with the torn piece of me
I had lent.

And then it was gone

a wisp of
mist curling from an
icy pond.

Boxes

Meaghan Calcari Campbell

I look around our house and we have a lot of boxes. A reclaimed Midwest milk crate that holds our cozy blankets. A bright yellow, red and green-painted tin from Taiwan full of loose leaf green tea. My grandpa's crumbling old cigar box that contains dusty photographs and sweet mementos from my grandparents' time in San Francisco during World War II.

Boxes hold elements of surprise and can be reminiscent of joyous times. A birthday or Christmas, perhaps.

Boxes can also conceal something, tucked away for safe-keeping.

One of my coping mechanisms incorporates these boxes of myriad shapes, sizes and colors. When I am stressed or something is happening over which I have no control, I pull out these boxes, in my mind at least, and place the worry in them. I close the lid tightly and put the box back on the shelf. Maybe I will never open it again. Or maybe I will open it in five minutes.

It is an exercise in self-constraint.

I have needed those boxes a lot lately.

I have been living with chronic back pain for several months.

It has continued to worsen with recent numbness radiating to my arms, hands and feet at times. My oncologist saw me immediately with this new development and ordered an MRI. Not wanting to alarm many people, I shared this with only a few co-workers. Then I told a friend from my support group. And finally, my husband Mike. We pretended it was not a big deal—maybe a slipped disc or pinched nerve, or the onset of osteoporosis in my spine because of my hormone therapy.

So I headed in for the MRI, to be a ninety-minute scan while laying perfectly still. I wanted to take Ativan to get through it, but had to drive to work to give a presentation right afterwards. Falling asleep on the interstate or drooling in front of the Board of Directors seemed ruinous in different ways.

I changed into the paper gown and the technician, Sylvio, got my IV started. As I laid down on the MRI table, he paused while reviewing my chart and asked, "As part of your breast cancer reconstruction, do you have a temporary tissue expander?" Me, "Yes." Sylvio, "You need to leave this room immediately!" Me, "Shit!"

Because the magnets are so incredibly strong in an MRI machine, a patient cannot have any metal on or in her body. It could get ripped out at worst, super hot at best, or shift around to rearrange some muscles and tissues in between. Because of my surgical complications during breast reconstruction, I have metal in my chest. But my doctor failed to remember this when she ordered the MRI.

Zoinks.

Cut to the next day and Mach 10 escalation, with a PET/CT as the next best diagnostic tool to determine if my cancer is hanging out in my spine. Being back in the PET/CT room, on that table in particular, the scene of my first PET/CT now years before, I had to pull out many boxes and put all my post-traumatic triggers and fears into them, slam them shut, put a lot of bricks on top, and throw a blanket over them. I was mentally and physically exhausted afterwards. And, radioactive, too. I was told not to hold small children.

Later that week as I waited for the scan results, I sat through my dear friend Erin's memorial, wondering to myself, why not me? Why her? And thinking that maybe my ticket was being pulled and I would soon be asking why me? Why did I go from no evidence of disease, after years of aggressive treatment, to metastatic?

Boxes, boxes, boxes.

The PET/CT results came back with no cancer. Good news for now, despite not having a diagnosis for the problem. All signs point to a perplexing combination of degenerative bone disease caused by the hormone therapy that put me into chemically-induced menopause, and the mastectomy shifting around my pectoral and back muscles.

Deep breath and/or kick something.

All of this reminds me of vulnerability. We are all vulnerable. Just because I feel good today does not mean it is guaranteed for tomorrow.

An excerpt of this poem came to me randomly the day of my PET/CT and says it all:

"Vulnerability is not a weakness, a passing indisposition, or something we can arrange to do without, vulnerability is not a choice, vulnerability is the underlying, ever present and abiding under-current of our natural state. To run from vulnerability is to run from the essence of our nature, the attempt to be invulnerable is the vain attempt to become something we are not and most especially, to close off our understanding of the grief of others. More seriously, in refusing our vulnerability we refuse the help needed at every turn of our existence and immobilize the essential, tidal and conversational foundations of our identity."

— David Whyte, "Vulnerability" from *Consolations: The Solace, Nourishment and Underlying Meaning of Everyday Words*

Boxes.
Vulnerability.
Boxes.

Fighting Words

Doreenda Ziba

Years ago, in a Criminal Law course, we discussed the concept of "fighting words." My professor mentioned that inciting words do not generally justify assault and battery. However, there is a grey area surrounding "fighting words." Some words are so hurtful and so cruel that even a reasonable person could react in a violent manner. The lecture ended there. But this idea has been something I have thought about throughout both my legal career and my personal journey with breast cancer.

I am a "fighter," "survivor," and "woman warrior." A "soldier" who "suffers from Post-Traumatic Stress Disorder (PTSD)." I am going to "beat" cancer. I am going to "win." These are all things that well-meaning people have said to me. I appreciate it. Sometimes I even use these types of words to describe myself, and the friends I have made in my cancer community.

For me, though, fighting words have been troublesome because they are often used to describe something that, in reality, my body is doing to me.

The question must be asked: what exactly are we "survivors"

fighting? It can only be our own selves. While I do not want to be defined as a "survivor," the truth is, I DO feel like I survived something. Perhaps though, it is more of an inner conflict rather than the disease itself.

I ask myself, what part of myself is me? Am I my body and my body attacked myself? If I am to love myself, am I to love all parts of myself? Including the cancerous cells that are a part of me? And, by extension, am I to love cancer? Is it that I am my mind and my body attacked me? Or, I am my body so I attacked myself? It is an existential crisis that I cannot resolve.

This murkiness begs the question: if the cancer is me, then am I fighting myself? Or, am I fighting rogue cancer cells that are not me? If they are not me, then where the hell did they come from? And really, is it me that is doing the fighting? Was it the chemotherapy that did the fighting as I sat on the sidelines letting it fight me? And then the chemo did not kill me, so that means I beat the chemo, which beat the cancer, which also beat me since it killed all my good white blood cells, too? Oh god, and then there is the surgery—did I have to cut off a part of myself to save the rest of myself and so, the cancer beat the breast, but I won the war? And later on, at this stage is it not the daily pill Tamoxifen that is doing all the work? My way of dealing with this lack of resolution is, "oh fuck it, who knows." This allows me to get on with life more easily.

We are so out of touch with ourselves that, in order to think about our own illness, we want to think of it as something outside of us that we must fight against. Although I have "beaten" cancer, I still feel like it is a part of me. Several of my loved ones do not want to come to terms with this. They want it to be over. In fact, some do not even say the word "cancer" to me. My father, who was my main caregiver and who I talk to everyday, has said the word "cancer" only once to me, in Farsi ("saraton"), really quickly, as though if he said it fast enough the whole thing would go away just as quickly. Or even more likely, it would be easier to pretend it was never said, never happened, to forget about it and look to the future.

Of course, there were some who, as much as they felt uncomfortable with the idea of me dying or being ill, were able to deal with those issues on their own and allow me to talk about it openly. My sister Amanda told me that she spoke with a friend who asked her why she could not think about me dying. Amanda answered that she just could not. Her friend suggested that she *should* think about it. Amanda did, with her friend's support. And Amanda told me she realized that her life would not end, but it would REALLY, REALLY suck, forever, because she would no longer have her little sister.

At first, it scared me that she thought my death was a possibility. But later, I realized that she had the same fears as I did and we could talk openly about these fears. The fact that they were not just MY fears, but OUR fears, meant that I was no longer carrying the burden on my own. We could talk about these fears and use all the scary language that no one wants to hear but is in my head nonetheless. Some people need to be reassured, sometimes falsely, but I need to feel like I am not alone with my fears.

When I was first diagnosed, the surgeon gave me a pamphlet entitled, "Information for Survivors." That term scared me. Hearing it meant that there was a chance I would not be a survivor, there would be casualties, I could actually fail to survive. And what about those who do die—are they not "survivors," and are thus failures? Am I making too much of these words? Do other "survivors" do this too? Or do they get cancer, become survivors, and get on with their lives? Why am I so obsessed with these words and their meanings? How can I find terms that I feel comfortable with? Are there other languages that have better words? Farsi, for the first time in my life, is lacking. Usually there is a word in Farsi that does not exist in English and that better defines and illustrates a feeling, act or gesture. But, now even Farsi fails me. Because my people are so scared of illness and death, we do not talk about it. We are in denial. As a child, the word "saraton" (cancer) was used only as a curse on *others*. "Saraton begeereh" (may s/he get cancer!). It was never used as a real thing that could happen to us. Now that I have had cancer, my mother had cancer, my uncle had cancer, I feel like the word should be freely bandied about in our family. But still, it is hush, hush. My mother "passed away" from it—in the past. My uncle and I "had" it—in the past.

I am, of course, glad it is in the past. I want it to stay there forever. Even writing about it now is scaring me. But, I also want the freedom to be able to talk about saraton and to find non-fighting words for it. Perhaps someday we will find better language than what we currently use to describe cancer. Can we find language that is less violent, less binary, less about fighting, battling, surviving or losing, and more about the honest truth of this disease? After all, coming to terms with cancer means coming to terms with the terms.

Fuck Silver Linings and Pink Ribbons

Lori Wallace

Before I was diagnosed with cancer, I found "silver lining" stories moving and insightful and did not mind pink ribbons. Then, I developed cancer and discovered the devastating reality that no one wants to talk about. Here is MY cancer truth:

I live in constant fear of recurrence. I watch treatment fail cancer friends. I grieve their loss, deeply, especially those with young children. It breaks my heart and makes me wonder if my family and I are next. I worry that I will die before my younger son is grown, that my older guys will raise him too macho, out of touch with his heart and feelings, that they will drift apart without me here to keep pulling them back together.

So many things are different after cancer, "after" being relative. There is no way to know who finishes treatment cancer-free and who does not, only time will tell. That said, treatment changes everything.

I have chemo brain. My IQ has dropped ten points, my brain has trouble "writing" new information into memory, and I cannot think straight under pressure, or when I get tired or upset. I can no longer trust my mind and intuition. I forget, get confused, struggle with anxiety, sadness, frustration and have a short temper. A neuropsychologist tested my cognitive function and said that I have sensory overload. Chemo has caused my brain to remain hyperaware, constantly on the verge of fight or flight. No wonder I am so damn tired!

Exhaustion is my constant companion. As a young, single mother, I held two part time jobs while going to college full-time. Now, just getting out of bed can be a struggle, but we manage to get out the door, somehow. Sometimes, we are even on time.

Much of my body is numb, post-surgeries. I have to shave my arm pits by sight because I cannot feel that part of my body anymore, but cancer drug shots administered to my abdomen do not hurt. Silver lining? No. My ovaries are gone, and without them, my skin is aging at hyper speed. I have hot flashes and cold flashes, my bones ache, my libido is shot, and my vagina is a desert. Treatment also gives me headaches, I am praying it is not metastatic disease to the brain.

What have I learned from cancer and treatment? That it is horrible and we need to start coordinating research. With over two billion (with a "b") spent on breast cancer research so far, we should have found the causes and cures by now. Fuck silver linings and pink ribbons. Cancer is not pretty and pink, it is brutal and devastating. Please stop telling me to look on the bright side and be thankful to be alive.

Before cancer, I gave thanks all day. Thanks for green lights, shaded parking spaces, finding a jacket in the car when I forgot to bring one, just enough milk left for my coffee, living in such a beautiful place, having so many people that I love and love me. Now, I have to remind myself to be thankful. It does not bubble up naturally, like it did. I miss that.

I miss moving without discomfort. I miss feeling smart and hardworking and useful and energetic. I miss being the person I was before cancer.

I miss my previous life. I am not more spiritual, I already was before cancer. I am not more involved in my community, I was very involved before cancer. I am not more thankful for life, I was already thankful for everything in my life. Nothing good has come from cancer. Nothing. There is no silver lining. My wish is for people to stop trying to turn this devastation into a positive learning experience. It is not. It is another hardship I have to endure.

Maybe, someday, I will get used to this scarred, scatterbrained and faded version of me. Better yet, maybe someday, I will feel like my old self. Until then, I will TRY to be thankful for every laugh, hug and kiss. And for other things too.

That is, if my chemo brain allows me to remember.

Am I Doing It Right?

Meaghan Calcari Campbell

Breast cancer at thirty-two was the lamest birthday gift ever. After three rounds of chemo, multiple biopsies and surgeries, radiation, shots, and pills, I now have "no evidence of disease." It is the inapt clinical term for being, at least for now, cancer-free.

It is inaccurate because evidence of disease is all over me. It is part of me, a passenger, several chapters in my life story that left a trail of physical and emotional carnage—mastectomy incisions, port catheter stitches, biopsy scars, radiation tattoos, injection bruises, night sweats, and nightmares.

The most common question I get asked by well-meaning onlookers is, "How have you changed your life since cancer?"

Really?

Like, really?

Are you saying that in addition to having survived cancer, its treatments, and its million and one insults—including, but not limited to: diarrhea and constipation (often in the same day), nausea and vomiting, constant snot, joints that move like the tin man, fingernails jumping ship, blurred vision, getting felt up by well-meaning medical students in a gown as thin as ancient papyrus, manual dexterity that leaves me unable to open a soda can, twenty pounds of chemically-induced menopausal weight gain, mutilated body parts, and a chemo brain that seems to be functioning only on one cylinder—I now have to do something with my life and make meaning of it all? Surviving is not enough? I have to run a marathon and do it under four hours? Launch a different career that has me striding confidently down Market Street in high heels? Eat kale salads and avoid consuming cheddar cheese like it is the plague? Do yoga and acupuncture and meditation...all in the same day? Create a detailed, ambitious bucket list?

The implication of this question is that because of something I did or did not do, I gave myself cancer. It also suggests that you, the asker, will be OK because you will presumably be doing everything right, everything differently than me, such that you will be immune to "The Big C." It makes my blood boil because there is no immunity, there is only denial.

But, the bigger implication of this question is that there is a right and wrong way to "do" cancer. Like fight, be strong, have faith, be brave, stay upbeat, keep a positive attitude, put it behind you, move on, it is over, you are cured right, be grateful, at least you are alive.

What if my answer to the question of how I have changed my life is that I now prefer to lay on the couch and watch reality TV, eat hamburgers, globe trot through cheese tastings, drink beer, strong beer, stay in my same job and get fat and wear yoga pants every day?

And what if I told you that instead of a bucket list, I have created a fuck-it list?

That is right. I am getting rid of the anxiety and perpetually unmet expectations that others put on me and I put on myself. The fuck-it list says that *this* is what I will let go of and will not do in the world.

The fuck-it list includes just saying "fuck it" to things like loving running, or even liking running, or even just running, learning a second language, wearing high heels on Market Street, applying for new jobs tomorrow, attaining perpetual loving-kindness, always saying "Yes," being at one with the universe, and feeling guilty about eating hamburgers and cheese and drinking beer…lots of beer. Wine, too. Fuck it.

Maybe the savvy reader is thinking—"A-ha! You did change your life."

I did.

Not because of cancer, but in spite of cancer. And, not because you asked.

Not Pink

Jessica Les

Among mounds of fresh red and green chilies, I encountered the first rack of pink grocery bags. October had arrived and I was back in Albuquerque piecing my life together. I felt a tinge of pain, I think somewhere near my spleen. Is that where memory lives? I gripped the grocery cart handle and moved toward the broccoli crowns.

A woman's voice melodically spilled from a speaker above the yams, "Good morning shoppers. Breast cancer awareness pink dahlias on sale for $14.99." I reached resolutely for the brussels sprouts.

"One percent of all Activia yogurt proceeds will support breast cancer." I pushed on towards the berries. Surely the last of the season, I splurged and grabbed four pints.

"Thank you for shopping at Sunflower Market, your neighborhood store committed to Breast Cancer Awareness Month." I grit my teeth.

I continued to fill my cart with anti-oxidant-rich red peppers, selenium-packed Brazil nuts, and lycopene-rich tomatoes. I passed another stand of pink breast cancer awareness bags tacked to a

147

crate of pumpkins. Stay focused. I paused and reviewed my cart, mentally comparing it to the anti-cancer chart a nutritionist gave me last fall when I was being treated for breast cancer. I had always been a healthy eater, but since I was diagnosed at age twenty-eight, nutrition had become a religion.

This week is no different than the last, I told myself. The fresh fruits and vegetables piled in my cart, the same.

Normally I filled with pride in the produce section, for taking such good care of myself, for doing everything I could to keep cancer away. But today leaving the zucchini area, my stomach lurched then turned itself over. I want out of here. Each pink ribbon and grocery bag was a reminder of the painful moments when I realized life was wildly unfair. Like in eighth grade, when I tried to stop two big boys from teasing my friend, Fareeda, for the fine hair on her upper lip. Instead of halting the boys, the bus driver kicked Fareeda and me off the bus and made us walk the rest of the way home in the dingy February snow.

Like that bus ride, cancer was something I would rather forget. Seeing my parents crumple with the news. The unclean surgical margins. My mangled chest. The spinning nausea of treatment. The stale taste of uncertainty.

The stupid pink bags made forgetting impossible. I gripped the shopping cart handle and took a deep breath. "I am OK. I am here," I told myself.

I got in line at the grocery checkout. I scanned the magazine rack for distraction but instead saw a pink sign that read, "178,480 U.S. women were diagnosed with invasive breast cancer last year. 40,460 died from the disease."

My forehead flushed and my palms began to sweat. Another deep breath. I blindly unloaded my produce, my protection, on the conveyer belt. The cashier, wearing a pink t-shirt with a giant ribbon stamped on the chest asked if I would like a list of this month's breast cancer events.

"No," I muttered as I turned my attention to bagging my groceries. I loaded cherry tomatoes, avocados, spinach, chard, cantaloupe and yams into my own mesh bag bearing Frida Kahlo's portrait in clashing pink, green and red. This bag I brought from home, was now filled with healing leaves, fruits and tubers. Suddenly my eyes were wet, blurring the buttons on the debit card machine.

"Miss. Hello, Miss?" It was the cashier again. "Miss, you pressed the wrong buttons. Please pay again." The automatic door bowed open before me. A wiry old man scuffled his cowboy boots across the parking lot. His threadbare jeans were worn the color of the sky. An uneven blue. A toddler being loaded into a cart squealed "daw-gie" and flapped his legs while pointing at a border collie barking from a pickup truck across the lot. Out here, nothing was breast cancer pink, there were no ribbons. The rustle of sycamore leaves from the edge of the parking lot replaced the

149

bleating breast cancer awareness messages. My arms were strong. They easily lifted Frida Kahlo into the trunk of my car. Although the bulbous produce she contained distorted her face, her eyes were unchanged. Stern, elegant and knowing. Out there in the parking lot with Frida in my trunk, I realized I stood anonymously with my antioxidants. The irritated patch of memory nestled next to my spleen loosened, no longer exquisitely painful. I got in my car and drove away.

VII. POST-SCRIPT

"I can't go on, I'll go on."

— Samuel Beckett, *The Unnamable*

"Until I cease to breathe, I will."

— David Menasche, *The Priority List: A Teacher's Final Quest to Discover Life's Greatest Lessons*

A Choice

Emily Kaplan

who chose this life
not that other person's
or the one we dreamed of

I did not choose this coat
Erin did and it became mine
not my choice but hers worn with love in the cold

my eggs cook
I look at the pan and think of Jane
her choice not mine
not her choice to leave the pan to me

Sarah

Emily Kaplan

she died on this day
we found out at the same time
that breast cancer was back

mine was local straight
located in the muscle
fight it hard chemo survive

hers further along
pain in fear and scared for life
mets diagnosis

both with girl and boy
too unbearable to leave
blonde locks and big eyes

why her now not me
can I explain to others
this woman is me

Ennui, Part I and II

IPJ

Part I.

Letdown. Anticlimax. Apathy. I fought for my life and I won. Now what?

When I was first diagnosed with metastatic cancer and undergoing treatment, I had it down. I did yoga and meditated. I spent time with friends. I communicated openly. I tried to have a baby, unsuccessfully. I ate well, took supplements, and drank, well, about the same. I went on ridiculous vacations, rock climbing in Thailand and snowboarding in New Zealand, Argentina and Japan. I took time off work because I was going to die, fuck it! I dated bad boys because it did not matter, I did not have a future for which to provide. I spent five years doing mostly whatever I wanted, because it was fun, meaningful, and important to me.

But recently, I lost my mojo, my Zen-like calm. It has been four years since my last cancer recurrence. Now I am consumed by work, which I love, but I have lost my balance, my joie de vivre.

Going from metastatic breast cancer to no evidence of disease was hard-fought. After chemotherapy, a mastectomy, radiation, more chemo, and two liver resections, cancer is gone. It took a few years for me to accept, to think about maybe having a future again, and it is scary, after having let it go. My prognosis was two years to live. Now I have a life sentence…to live. I have to think about aging and retirement. And forever. But, how can I hold on to that appreciation I had for each day, each moment, the smell of each flower?

One thing I have not let go of is my breast cancer support group. My non-cancer friends ask me, "Why do you still hang out with those cancer people? You don't have cancer anymore, let it go. Besides, they keep dying and bringing you down." Because these remarkable beautiful wonderful women are my people. I have been where they are, and I am going where they are going. They are my thread of a connection to that deeper appreciation. Maybe they are my answer. They remind me that the small moments are precious, and life is short. Someday, when my shit hits the fan again, they will be there for me.

I have been to a lot of their funerals, memorials, and celebrations of life. I have also been privileged to hold many newborn babies. The cycle of life keeps on rolling. Yet I feel removed from it all, surgically separated. I cannot have children, and I am not imminently dying. It is a sort of limbo, a numbness. I come back to the question humans have been asking since the beginning of time: Why am I here? Why did I survive? Is there some greater purpose or just dumb luck?

We have a duty and honor in this cancer world and support

group to tread closely with death. We carry the memories of our friends who have gone before us. We travel together towards the end so that none of us goes alone. We know this path better than most. We do not ask "How long will this treatment be?" We take the treatment as long as it works, despite the discomfort and side effects. With metastatic cancer, it is a marathon, not a sprint. My cancer is never really gone; it just waits for me to let down my guard so it can take over my body.

I have been living in a free space, the eye of my metastatic cancer storm, flirting with the word "cure." I must find a way to enjoy and appreciate it. Meanwhile, my dear friends fight battles every day. Battles to get out of bed, to eat food, and they try to enjoy life such as it is. Is every day really a gift? No. Some days are a living hell. I have watched many friends realize they are dying. How do I hold them? How do I sit with them and tell them it will be OK? I do not know, I just try my best.

Part II.

Ennui is short-lived and appears absurd in my rearview mirror.

My cancer is back, fifteen tumors littering my liver. The first treatment did not work, so on to the next. I am on the hunt for the one that will work, will put me back into remission. Or just give me a few more months. How long will I be in treatment? The rest of my life.

I visited a friend in hospice last week. She died a few days later. She had metastatic breast cancer. I have metastatic breast cancer.

When I visited her I said, "I'm so sorry." She said, though she could barely speak, "Sorry why?" I could not answer.

I am sorry you are dying. I am sorry for your children. I am sorry for those you leave behind. But she was not sorry, she was not in pain, her loved ones were present, she accepted what was happening. She said, in those words, not to be sorry for her. To accept the cycle of life as she had.

We all are on this long slow march to the end. From birth, the walk begins. But it is awful to literally see and feel the tumors growing. To know the end is coming, sooner than we had thought.

My dear friend, Merijane Block, also living with metastatic breast cancer, wrote in April, 1992:
"Everything takes longer
Than you think it should
Or thought it would
Except your life."

Elegy for Lenore

Erin Williams Hyman

"Open closed open. Before we are born, everything is open
in the universe without us. For as long as we live, everything is
closed within us. And when we die, everything is open again.
Open closed open. That's all we are."

— Yehuda Amichai, "The precision of pain and the
blurriness of joy: the touch of longing is everywhere" from
Open Closed Open

I love this piece of poetry and I think about it all the time—the
way before our existence we are part of the limitless pulse of
energy, and how we are returned to it after the short parenthesis
that is our individual, bounded life. In this vision, death is like a
new breath, a universal exhale, a release back into the all.

Lenore Lefer taught me how to die. Which is to say, she
taught me and twelve other young women with cancer how to live
while dying—which is what we are *all* doing, by the way, cancer
or no. I met her at a weekend retreat at Commonweal, an
extraordinary organization that runs Cancer Support Retreats that
coax you out of your shell of grief and shock, appeal to what you

most want your life to be about, and by helping you envision it, bring it into being, for whatever time you have.

It is potent stuff.

I drove up the long dirt driveway in my long blonde wig, only days out of my chemo session, to their perch in an old radio building on the bluffs above the beach. I was looking forward to the yoga, to the time with women I knew well and not so well, to being cooked for and taken care of for the weekend. I thought I was feeling and doing pretty well "holding it together." The kids were just back in school after our family had taken a wonderful road trip up the West Coast to Vancouver. I was ready to turn the page.

This, despite the fact that I knew that the chemo had only been partially successful. There were still recalcitrant tumors in my liver that had hunkered down and ridden out the storm. And this was a secret to most. Not yet ready to be public with the fact that my cancer would not be curable, I was putting on a "yes-it's-great-that-it's-over" face, not knowing any other way to protect myself, too vulnerable to let myself be seen as a tragic figure.

In our session with Lenore, she did something I have never seen any therapist do: she let down with us; she let us into her own pain.

She had white hair, wide compassionate eyes, and the mouth of a lipstick model. Her beauty, in her seventies, reminded me of both of my grandmothers, now passed, who never sought to eliminate their wrinkles, but saw them only ever as laugh lines and sparkled always all the more for deeply inhabiting the experience written on their faces. She spoke with an East Coast accent, having grown up Jewish in New York, but one moderated by many years in California, with a throaty softness. She came, she said from a "cancer family," and the scourge in its numerous forms had claimed many members. She also told us about losing her youngest son as a teenager when he drowned at Big Sur. Even though it had happened decades before, and even though she surely had shared that information with other groups, she was choked up in the telling. The grief never recedes.

The topic of our discussion that day has not only stayed with me, but is something I carry constantly with me, and remove from my pocket like a worry rock or a talisman, something to bring to mind on a regular basis. What is your soul calling you to do? What is the mission, the meaning, only you can fulfill? Where have you hidden away your most profound desires and aspirations? Can you unearth them? Most importantly, how are you actively thwarting their accomplishment? Yes, that is the challenge—figuring out all the ways we work against ourselves.

Lenore gave an example of a time in her career, twenty years earlier, when no one was teaching or discussing the profound implications for sexuality after cancer treatment. Many treatments can leave both men and women infertile or impotent, or with life-long challenges for physical intimacy. No one at the time was talking about it. Lenore had done so much therapeutic work with people on the topic, had researched everything she could get her hands on, and she knew that she was being "called" to teach on this topic. But she was standing in her own way. Because she had a terrible fear of public speaking. Either she had to abandon this soul mandate, or she had to find a way to break through her own blockage, her own terrible apprehensions.

We all do this to ourselves. The thing we want most is the thing that carries the greatest risk of failure, the most acute threat to our competence, our OK-ness. One woman in our group had a passion for photography, but instead of doing her own work, her job was selling the work of other photographers. I related to that one myself; why was I spending my time as an editor, making everyone else's half-assed writing sound polished instead of being a writer myself? We so assiduously sabotage the very thing that would bring us the most satisfaction: "I can't now...I'm too busy...It won't work...I have to...I can't."

Each woman in the circle took some time to excavate what that soul-calling might be. Having a baby. Reuniting with a lost love. Finishing a degree. Reconciling with a mother. Each one could count the myriad roadblocks they, themselves, had placed in the path of each of these things.

In an evening session later that day with Lenore, she asked us to speak directly about our fears about death. What in it was most fearful—pain? Suffering? Or extinction itself? My composure dissolved on the spot; I started weeping and was unable to stop for the next several hours. My wig was long gone by this point, my hairless head, and eyelash-less eyes making the stream of grief seem all the more unadulterated. Every time I thought of my children it was unbearable; I could not get any air.

Later, in a quieter moment, Lenore approached me to see how I was doing. She put a hand on my shoulder and looked deeply into my eyes; red-rimmed, still watery, I wanted to avert them, but her gaze stayed with me, would not look away. When I said I was shocked at how much had come out, she said, "Just think of all the energy it's been taking for you to hold that back."

Although I only spent time with her over that one weekend, I felt a bond with Lenore that I cannot explain. I can call up her presence as if she were someone I knew deeply. If I were one to believe in past lives, I would say we had known each other in another dimension; I do not believe in such things, but such was the power of her soulful presence to me.

After leaving Commonweal, I longed to repeat the experience, or to have someone like Lenore in my life on a regular basis, guiding me to traverse my grief, not shy away from it, encouraging me to shun the voices that say, "You can't" when my soul calls. Finally, I thought, well, maybe Lenore would take me as an individual client. I called to find out.

She would have, but she was not taking individual clients anymore—or any clients—for she had just learned that she herself had inoperable pancreatic cancer. I was stunned; I cried and raged and kicked shit around the house. Lenore chose not to have chemotherapy (which would not have done much good and would have produced much suffering) and to spend her final months with her family and loved ones.

I know this too, because I got to witness some of it in the form of a documentary called *Time of Death*. It turns out that after a lifetime of counseling people on how to come to terms with death, Lenore made the ultimate generous gift of allowing all of us, anyone, to witness her own.

It was not something I could watch alone; four other women who had participated in the weekend retreat came to watch it together. We got to "meet" Mel, Lenore's husband of fifty-three years, and her two sons, and grandchildren. Lenore starts the film so cogent in her motives—"we live in a death-denying culture"— and it begins with her throwing a Farewell Party to begin to say goodbye to the people in her life. But despite her immense, unfathomable courage, it was still painfully difficult to watch her fade in strength, in clarity, becoming restricted to her bed with only her intimates around her. Still, she shone with love. Her final words, lying in her husband's arms, were "it's been terrific."

A Life Well-Lived

MEF

It was official, the proverbial other shoe, which had been hanging precariously from my fingers, had dropped. The cancer I had been holding at bay had now spread to my lungs. This came after watching my sister die from the same disease that was now setting up camp in more parts of my body. Following my initial paralyzing fear and anger and the knowledge my next course of treatment would not be easy, I did the next best thing I could do with such life-altering news—I booked a three week trip to Australia and we left two weeks later. Treatment would start as soon as I got back but until that time, I would swim in the Great Barrier Reef and watch the sun rise and set on Uluru Rock.

I made many memories with my husband and son on that trip. I have been making as many as I can since my cancer spread in 2007. To me, life is about experiences, and travel is my passion.

The sun rising on Haleakala, backpacking through Europe for a month with my husband, listening to howler monkeys as I fall asleep in a Costa Rican rainforest. The joy of showing my son where to get the best almond croissant in Paris, before heading to the top of the Eiffel Tower. I remember how wide his eyes got when he saw Michelangelo's *David* for the first time. The thrill of zip-lining in Honduras and climbing the Mayan ruins. I remember the six summers it took us to travel to every Major League Baseball stadium. I embraced the pouring rain as we cheered the San Francisco Giants to the pennant.

I relish the simpler things in life as well. I listen to the birds in the trees and feel the sun on my face when I go for a walk. I squish the sand between my toes as I watch the waves crash upon the shore. I listen to the beautiful sound of my son's laughter and welcome the butterflies I still get when my husband gives me that certain smile, even after twenty-five years. I surround myself with the laughter of my friends and good wine. I savor every morsel of that perfect piece of dessert. I already know that life is too short not to have dessert. I live because I can, because today I am here. Tomorrow is promised to no one. The memories are what keep me going to the chemotherapy infusion center every week, so I can make more of them. I live for my sister and the others who have gone before me, just as I hope others will do in my memory. I want a life well-lived, however long that life may be. And, I want a bounty of memories as I careen, battered and bruised, to my final resting spot.

VIII. EPILOGUE

The Feast

Ann Kim

Erin Williams Hyman was more than just a member of our support group, the Bay Area Young Survivors (BAYS). She was the mastermind and editor of our story first anthology, *The Day My Nipple Fell Off*. She was the hostess of our raucous and often racy holiday parties. Erin was the first to sign up for our physical challenge hikes and runs. And she helped to moderate our active online community—a place where our members can ask the questions that keep them up in the middle of the night.

One of the topics that comes up frequently and generates a lot of discussion is the relationship between cancer and food.

We have a lot of confusion: is soy a good thing or bad thing? What *do* I do with chia seeds? We have a lot of anger: I have been a vegetarian my whole life, so how is it fair that I got cancer? We have a lot of fear: will my cancer come back if I enjoy a glass of wine with dinner? And, we have a lot of sadness: food used to bring me such joy, but now that joy is gone.

Confusion, anger, fear, and sadness. The same feelings we all had when we learned of Erin's death at the all-too-young age of forty-two.

169

As I sat in mourning and contemplated Erin's legacy, I was reminded of something Erin wrote to our support group in response to a series of emails about cancer and food:

"I read the recent posts with so much consternation, so much sadness for the anxiety and the anger and the infuriating contradictions in 'recommendations.' I fight with all of it too and have been on every side of this debate, from my post-diagnosis juicing regimen (beets, carrots, fresh turmeric root!) to my full-throated refusal to give up yet another aspect of my life that matters to me. Sick of quinoa and green tea, I have thrown up my hands and said 'I can't live the rest of my life like I'm on a cleanse.'

But, I had a vision this morning. I want to sweep us all up—every one of us—and fly us to Italy. At least in our imaginations.

When I was in my twenties, I lived in Europe, and once, when my parents visited, we went together to Positano. This dramatic centerpoint of the Amalfi Coast is one of those dream-like towns with ice-cream colored houses impossibly stacked on each other, on steep cliffs down to the Mediterranean. One day, on the suggestion of a local, we hiked up, away from the town, even higher on the cliffs—up and up and up. We steadily climbed 1,742 stairs up to the peak, past tiny vegetable gardens wedged in between houses, olive groves and lemon trees on precipitous terraces, until we reached a tiny restaurant with a patio looking down over all we had climbed, the sea sparkling astonishingly far below.

To call it a 'restaurant' is actually a misnomer: do not think menus or waiters or even a cash register. It was really two or three rickety tables on the back patio of an Italian grandma, a 'nonna,' who was basically letting a few knowing strangers come over for lunch. You ate whatever she brought you, and you blessed every single morsel for the unbelievable tastes it emitted.

Can you picture this? If we were there, there would be no 'kosher,' no 'vegan,' no 'gluten-free.' She would not countenance putting anything 'on the side.' There would be squash blossoms picked that day, and pillows of pasta she rolled out on her counter that morning, and tomatoes that would make you think you had never before eaten a tomato in your life. There would be fish, grilled with spices and herbs so insane you would be sucking the bones for every last possible nibble because you did not want it to end. There would most certainly be wine, but washed down with a lot of water, and possibly some grappa at the end. When you finished this meal, pushing the chair back from the table with the sun on your face, every cell in your body would be singing with contentment. Then you would have to figure out how to get back down those 1,742 stairs.

Can you feel it? Can we remember that food is not medicine and food is not poison? It is nourishment we need, both body and soul. It is communal and it is pleasurable and it does not have the final word on our future.

I am not suggesting we spend all day in the kitchen. Far from it. Let us just love food more and torment ourselves less. Let us give thanks for the choices we have and try our best not to torture ourselves over them. Let us please remember that if we climb 1,742 steps, we deserve an incredible meal."

I have been with BAYS since it was formed over ten years ago, and I have seen many of our members die—by my count, thirty-five members, most of whom died in their twenties, thirties, or early forties. Some of them I only knew as a name from an email, but many of them—like Erin—I knew as friends and sisters.

People ask me how I cope with so much loss, and my answer may surprise you: these women are not dead to me. I see them in my dreams, feel them in my heart, and even talk to them on a regular basis. Most wonderfully, they speak to me, whisper things in my ear, inspire me to be more than I was.

Today, I hear Erin whispering in my ear. Here is what she is saying:

"Mourn me. Grieve for my family. And feel angry that my life ended too soon. And then, after you climb those rocky steps of despair, feast at the incredible table of life. Scream your lungs out when the San Francisco Giants win the World Series. Breathe deeply when you smell the head of a newborn baby. Sit down with your loved ones and share an amazing meal.

I will be right there with you."

In loving memory of Erin Williams Hyman. This story is adapted from the eulogy read at Erin's memorial service on October 19, 2014—two days before the start of the World Series, in which the Giants won the Championship in Game Seven.

CONTRIBUTOR PROFILES

Nola Agha
A native Californian, Nola is a world traveler, musician, sports economist, and was voted "Most Likely to be in the Olympics" her senior year in high school. She was diagnosed with Stage IIIC breast cancer only a few months after starting her dream job as a professor at the University of San Francisco—she was thirty-five and her children were two and three. With the help of her friends, family, and loving high-school-sweetheart husband, Nola won her struggle with cancer. Recently, she climbed Mt. Whitney (the tallest peak in the continental United States) to say "F*** you" to cancer. In her spare time you can find her driving kids to piano and judo, petting her cat, and hiking in the woods.

Judith Basya
Judith writes the "What's Wrong With You" advice column for HeebMagazine.com, where she is also Literary Editor. A Manhattanite transplanted to California more than once by her husband, they are currently enjoying the San Francisco Bay Area with their two daughters. She was diagnosed with cancer at forty and again at forty-four and looks forward to finishing chemo exactly one week from the day she is penning this bio. She is not looking forward to Tamoxifen, though, because she tried it last time and it made her uncontrollably angry. You can find her easily on Facebook, Twitter and at JudithBasya.com, where perhaps she will pour her impending rage into a blog. Do not be scared—she is usually friendly.

Meaghan Calcari Campbell
Meaghan has roots in small-town Illinois and now calls San Francisco home. She works in philanthropy and ocean conservation with local communities and non-profits. Diagnosed with breast cancer at thirty-two without a family history of the disease, her initial treatments lasted sixteen months and will now continue for many years. Meaghan finds great joy in serving as

175

President of the Bay Area Young Survivors (BAYS), and her essays were published in the first BAYS book, *The Day My Nipple Fell Off.* She has traveled to twelve countries and paddled three rivers since her diagnosis in 2012, and looks forward to more adventures with her husband Mike and dear friends. To see more of Meaghan's writing, visit http://keepingabreast.me/.

Roxanne Cohen
Roxanne is a native New Yorker who has called the San Francisco Bay Area home for over fifteen years. Through her two-time cancer journey, Roxanne has managed not only to survive, but also to thrive. Since completing treatments, she has run three half marathons, performed as Mamma Ogre in a community theater production of Shrek, and has continued to work full time in philanthropy. She is a proud mother of two amazing and resilient children, and is celebrating her twentieth wedding anniversary this Fall. She feels blessed by the remarkable community, dearest of friends and devoted family whose love and support have enabled her to be where she is today.

Sarah Haberfeld de Haaff
Sarah never fancied herself a writer, but fell into it by way of her breast cancer experience. She worked with young children as a speech pathologist in San Francisco. Diagnosed initially in August 2011, she tackled chemotherapy, a bilateral mastectomy, and radiation, all while potty-training one child, Gabe, and preparing the other, Sophia, for kindergarten. Sarah was diagnosed with metastatic disease in August 2013. She readily admitted that she could live life so fully because of her husband Greg and family and friends in their amazing circle around her. Throughout her surreal journey, she carried herself with dignity, humor, openness, warmth, bravado and determination. She taught us all what it means to live with integrity, even through suffering. Sarah died from metastatic breast cancer on February 23, 2015 at the age of forty.

Wendy Donner
Wendy is an educational consultant and writer living in Marin. She is currently working on an educational research project focused on maker-centered learning. Wendy found writing her blog, <u>We GOT This,</u> to be an invaluable tool during her cancer treatment and her pieces have been featured on the *Huffington Post* and *Momastery*. In her free time, she can be found riding her bike up the Marin hills and romping around with her husband, two children, and rescue poodle, Star. To see more of her writing,
visit <u>www.wendydonner.com</u>.

MEF
MEF was born and raised in San Francisco and has lived her entire life in the Bay Area. She married her high school sweetheart and was fortunate enough to have an amazing son before she was diagnosed with breast cancer in 2003. MEF has been battling Stage IV breast cancer since 2007, so her primary job aside from being a mom, is managing treatments and various doctor's appointments, while dreaming of all the places she still has yet to visit.

Nancy Fawson
Nancy is a former attorney turned freelance writer, blogger and Managing Editor of the Southern Marin Mother's Club magazine, *The Crier*. She lives in the Bay Area with her husband, son Leo and daughter Sidney. She is cancer-free and healthy post-surgery and urges all women to be proactive in their own healthcare and do self-breast exams. You can read more of Nancy's work on her blog, <u>www.nycgirlbythebay.com</u>.

Rebecca J. Hogue
Rebecca is an itinerant scholar and prolific blogger. Professionally, she programs eLearning modules (Articulate Storyline), helps develop and produce self-published eBooks, and teaches Emerging Technologies and Instructional Design online. Her research and innovation interests are in the areas of online collaboration, social media, and blogging. You can read more of Rebecca's work at <u>http://rjh.goingeast.ca/</u>, <u>http://bcbecky.com</u>, <u>http://goingeast.ca/blo g.</u>

Cat Huegler
A huge sports fan and lover of anything (or anyone) fun, Cat was diagnosed with breast cancer in April of 2013, one month before her wedding. She did not postpone the wedding, marrying her best friend and having the time of their lives. Cat is from Reading, Pennsylvania, transplanted to the San Francisco Bay Area in 2006, and is now representing Oakland. She is former college athlete and coach, in both track and basketball. Cat works in tech. When she is not on a conference call, she is reading, napping, working out, planning a trip, or organizing fun for friends and family. Cat's cancer was detected at a routine check-up with her OB/GYN at the age of thirty-five. After a double mastectomy, six rounds of chemo, Herceptin, and about three million needle pricks, Cat is currently coping with hormone suppression yet not slowing down one bit.

Erin Williams Hyman
Erin was an editor of arts publications, the mother of two amazing boys, wife of a loving and intellectually-matched Rabbi, and a fierce Scrabble competitor. Her previous life as a Lit professor made her passionate about storytelling in all its forms. She believed that speaking the truth about our lives is essential to healing. More of her writing can be found at bmatzav.blogspot.com. Erin was the curator and editor of the first BAYS book, *The Day My Nipple Fell Off*. Erin was and is a model of strength, elegance and grace. With great magnanimity, purpose and fierce intellectual inquisitiveness, she lived and loved fully. Erin died from metastatic breast cancer on September 18, 2014 at the age of forty-two.

IPJ
IPJ fancies herself an athlete; she snowboards, rock climbs, practices yoga, and hikes. She also loves music and dancing. She was diagnosed with breast cancer at age thirty-two, metastatic at thirty-four. She then had four years without cancer, but is now fighting for her life.

Lochlann Jain
Lochlann is an Associate Professor of Anthropology at Stanford University. She is the author of *Malignant: How Cancer Becomes Us* (University of California Press: 2013), which won several prizes. www.lochlannjain.com

Emily Kaplan
Emily just passed year two since her second diagnosis of breast cancer. You may have seen Emily featured in the Scar Project, a series of large-scale portraits of young breast-cancer survivors. Visit the Project at www.thescarproject.org. Having turned her passion for wine into a career, she enjoys traveling to experience the wine and food culture of other countries. She ran the New York City Marathon in November, 2014, just because her body could. She lives in Berkeley with her husband and two kids, Samara, nine, and Micah, seven.

Ann Kim
As the daughter of a doctor, Ann grew up thinking that she would follow in her father's footsteps. When she realized that she could not stand the sight of blood, however, Ann pursued a career in law. As a founding board member and past President of BAYS, Ann feels grateful to fulfill her childhood dream of helping people through illness, just in a different way than she had originally planned.

Jessica Les
Jessica is a Wisconsin-born family doctor, doggie-momma, crafter and award-winning writer who gave breast cancer a run for its money both at age twenty-eight and thirty-three. Her writing has been featured in *Pulse, Literature and Medicine, Narrative Inquiry in Bioethics* and *Sonoma Medicine*. She is currently working on a book, *Navigating Illness*.

DM
DM was diagnosed with breast cancer a few weeks after her thirty-sixth birthday. Her treatment included surgery, chemotherapy and

radiation, and she is now taking Tamoxifen. She is grateful to her Oakland housemates; her family, dear friends, therapists, teachers and medical professionals on two coasts; and many others for their love and support. She began her breast cancer experience with a lot of questions and inspiration for art and change; and she made media art and wrote poems during the intensive portions of her treatment. Daily hormone therapy and fear of recurrence have slowed her down in humbling ways. She looks forward to speaking up more as she moves on, and she is so thankful for this anthology and the many, many ways it nurtures and supports us coming together and finding our voices.

Jenni Mork
Jenni is a longtime resident of San Francisco. She has written and performed in the San Francisco Bay Area focusing around issues of disability and sexuality. She loves to travel and has an ability to make any hotel an erotic wonderland or a writing retreat. The travails of navigating between continuing after-effects of breast cancer treatments and living in the today is her everyday project.

Ariana E. Nash
Ariana was born and raised in Montana and has been living in the San Francisco Bay Area since 1994. She enjoys writing, creating collages, practicing Pilates, and vintage clothing and furniture from the 1920's–1970's. What Ariana loves most about living in San Francisco is the knowledge that even after living in the city for over two decades, there are still new things to see and discover. She currently volunteers as a facilitator for the Young Survival Coalition, an organization that provides educational resources to young women affected by breast cancer. Ariana hopes that her two year-old niece, Abigail, will only have to read about breast cancer in history books and hopes she is still alive to answer any questions her niece has about it.

Laura Pexton
Laura loves adventures and laughter with friends and family. She has had a fulfilling career in the medical field as a nurse practitioner with a doctorate degree in nursing. She has traveled to

over forty countries and has participated in eleven humanitarian medical missions to far flung places. She was diagnosed with breast cancer in 2001 at age twenty-eight, just after her daughter was born. She has been in treatment for metastatic breast cancer since 2004. Her message to others is to live life beyond limits! One person CAN make a difference.

Laurie Hessen Pomeranz
Laurie is a San Francisco–based marriage, family and child therapist, who works with teen-aged boys and their parents. She is a proud mom of a teen-aged boy, and a grateful partner in a seventeen-year marriage. Laurie is a singer and dancer with a local tot-rock band, and she moonlights as a stylist with a multi-national jewelry company. She is in her happy place when she is watching her son, or the San Francisco Giants, play baseball. Laurie's writing has appeared in *Salon.com*, and in the anthologies *The Day My Nipple Fell Off* and *I Am With You.*

Andrea Ghoorah Sieminski
Andrea lives in San Francisco's Mission District with her husband, daughter and dog. Prior to becoming a stay at home mom, she practiced corporate law for major law firms as well as a Bay Area startup company. She was diagnosed with Stage I triple negative breast cancer in October of 2012 and concluded her treatment in July of 2013. To see more of her writing visit http://www.huffingtonpost.com/andrea-ghoorah-sieminski/ and comfortablynumb.co.

Marla Stein
Marla, her younger sister, mother and maternal grandmother are all breast cancer survivors who do not carry any known genetic mutations. Because she listened to her gut and advocated for herself, Marla found her lump at an early stage. Due to her age, she underwent chemotherapy and a bilateral mastectomy. As an advocate, Marla has previously served on Breast Cancer Action's Board of Directors and worked for the Breast Cancer Fund. Marla also mentors a teen girl through a local non-profit and enjoys volunteering. For fun, she spends quality time with her friends,

takes her dog to the beach and always has her passport ready to go! Originally from New York, Marla is thrilled to call San Francisco home.

Afroz Subedar

Afroz is a born and raised San Francisco Bay Area native. At the age of thirty-two, she found her own one cm lump by self-exam. She enjoys spending quality time with her husband, family, friends, colleagues and support group sisters. Afroz's interests include travelling, trying new restaurants, and finding ways to stay physically active. She is a forever faithful forty-niner fan and reality TV show junky. Afroz has a Master's of Science in Nutrition and is a Registered Dietitian and Certified Diabetes Educator.

Elodia Villaseñor

Elodia has spent the last decade doing either direct work or research in the area of youth development and Latin@ youth sexuality. Elodia is especially motivated by the strength and knowledge of youth and advocates for increasing visibility and voice for Latin@ youth while always working towards social justice. At home, Elodia has the joy and challenge of raising two strong chicas: Itzia, eleven, and Maya, four. They provide a daily reminder that with love and gratitude, one can move through anything. Elodia was diagnosed with Stage IIB triple negative breast cancer at the age of thirty-four. She lives in San Francisco.

Lori Wallace

Lori, a San Jose, California native, was diagnosed with early stage breast cancer a week before her youngest son's fifth birthday. She believed that treatment would take her out of commission for a few months, maybe a year, and then she would be "back in the game," trying to save the world while raising her two boys and loving her crazy family. That did not work out. Treatment was crippling and recovery was slow. Soon after returning to work, she found a new lump. Her cancer had progressed to Stage IV, metastatic disease, with no cure and median survival being two to three years. Lori is now forty-four years old, with an awesome twenty-four-year-old son, Evan, and sweet nine-year-old son, Braden. She has redirected her passion for sustainability and local community to breast cancer activism and is living condensed, squeezing as much fun as possible between rounds of chemo, loving family, friends and life even harder.

Anandi Wonder

Anandi is a forty-one year-old long-time San Franciscan queer, punk, and disability activist who believes that the breast cancer epidemic is but a symptom of the environmental destruction caused by this rotten system and cannot be cured without treating underlying causes—economic disparity and racial and gender oppression, for example. Despite the subject matter of her piece in this anthology, she actually prefers urban areas and spends the majority of her time happily taking photos of and appreciating buildings and signs with not a scrap of nature in sight.

Robin Bruns Worona

Robin is a San Francisco Bay Area copywriter and mother of twins. While her words frequently and successfully compel grownups to buy things, they have proven disappointingly unpersuasive on toddlers. She is always been better at writing than speaking, so she hopes things will change once her kids learn to read. Robin has lived in San Francisco with her amazingly supportive husband for nearly two decades and, as much as she loves it, she still misses the warm summer nights and twinkling fireflies of her native Rhode Island.

Kristen Nicole Zeitzer

Kristen was raised in Philadelphia and now calls Marin County home. Diagnosed with Stage III breast cancer in June 2014, she tackled surgery, chemotherapy, and radiation while working full-time and caring for her adorable son, Xander. Kristen designs strategic generics programs for a pharmaceutical wholesaler in San Francisco. She earned her BA from UCSD in Mathematics with a minor in Literature. On the weekends, you can usually find her hiking, taking Pilates classes in her loudest patterned leggings, and savoring time with Xander (often involving trains) and friends. An avid traveler, Kristen and her boarding school besties are actively planning post-treatment adventures.

Doreenda Ziba
Doreenda enjoys walking on the beach, kayaking, and biking. She is not afraid to admit it—she likes watching TV in bed with a glass of wine and crackers. She currently teaches yoga and does pro bono work advocating for Iranian refugees. To see more of her writing visit sitforabit.mindpress.com.

"Find a bit of beauty in the world today. Share it. If you can't find
it, create it.
Some days this may be hard to do. Persevere."

— Lisa Boncheck Adams, http://lisabadams.com/. Lisa died from
metastatic breast cancer on March 6, 2015 at the age of forty-six.

ACKNOWLEDGMENTS

The editors would like to honor and remember our beloved sister, Erin Williams Hyman, who first envisioned this book. While she was not alive to complete it herself, she inspired us to make it a reality through the passion and belief she instilled in us.

We wish to express our deep gratitude to the authors, who courageously and unabashedly put their experiences on paper, for the benefit of us all.

We are grateful for the wisdom offered by the following poets, doctors, writers, sportscasters, painters, and teachers: David Whyte, Yehuda Amichai, Atul Gawande, Cheryl Strayed, Stuart Scott, Richard Diebenkorn, Samuel Beckett, David Menasche, and Lisa Boncheck Adams.

Lastly, we acknowledge all of the women of the Bay Area Young Survivors—those who have gone before us, and those who stand beside us.

Made in the USA
San Bernardino, CA
17 November 2016